Tender Voices

True Stories by Women on a Journey of Love

Heal My Voice, Inc
Santa Monica, California

Tender Voices: True Stories by Women on a Journey of Love

Published by:
Heal My Voice, Inc
Andrea Hylen
Santa Monica, CA 90401
www.healmyvoice.org

ISBN-13: 978-0692268858 (Heal My Voice)
ISBN-10: 0692268855

Editor: Andrea Hylen
Cover design by Karen Brand

Printed in the United States of America

A portion of the proceeds from the sale of this book will be donated to further the non-profit work of Heal My Voice.

Dedication

To the Courageous Lovers:

We see you. We know how big your hearts are and we feel you. We honor you for the difference you are making in the world with your love. One smile. One hug. One word at a time.

We encourage you to write your story now and to keep shining your light in your home, your community and the world.

Your voice matters.

Blessing

Kathleen Nelson Troyer

Love is universal. It is present in everything. There are countless definitions and expressions of love - pure agape love, romantic love, and the love a mother has for her children.

Fear is the opposite of love. It gives us the gift of contrast and provides us with the opportunity to choose.

When we choose love over fear we become part of a powerful force that is shifting our world today.

May the authors of this book be blessed. We bless your love, strength and beauty. We bless your courage to share your story and message of love. We see you as catalysts, warriors, and awakeners of love. We are grateful for you. May you be deeply blessed with love.

May the readers of this book be blessed. You have been guided here for a reason. It is no coincidence that this book has found its way into your hands. There is a message for you here. You will know it when you see it. You will feel it. Allow the message to strengthen, nurture and guide you.

May you be blessed with the knowing that you are deeply held and loved

May the messages of love in this book send ripples though out the universe and beyond.

So be it! And so it is!

Kathleen Nelson Troyer is the founder of Gently Moving Forward and CEO of Jigsaw Staffing Solutions, Inc. She works with organizations and individuals as a human resources consultant, trainer, coach and mentor. She has been studying human potential, psychology and transformation for the past 25 years. She holds master level certifications in coaching, NLP, and Ericksonian Hypnosis. She leads intensive individual and group retreats and facilitates family and systemic constellations. Kat lives in a seaside cottage with a magical garden about 25 miles south of San Francisco near Half Moon Bay, California with her fabulous husband John, their three cats and dog.
www.gentlymovingforward.net

TABLE OF CONTENTS

Part One: I AM Compassionate

Part Two: I AM Devoted

Part Three: I AM Generous

FOREWORD

Beth Terrence

We are living at a time on our planet when the energy of love is what is truly needed to create transformation and healing on all levels. It is clear that the systems of mind and logic have taken humanity as far as it can go in terms of living in harmony and that another force is needed if we are to achieve balance individually and collectively. The force needed is LOVE!

In 2003, I was in a process of major transformation in my own life. I was in a deep grief process. My mother had died the year before as well as another close relative; my marriage of 10 years was crumbling. I had moved to another state for my husband's work and was struggling to rebuild my own business and earn a living. I had no foundation to stand on and the feelings of loss and grief I was experiencing were overwhelming.

Although there was an intensity to those immediate experiences, I also knew that the pain I was feeling was far greater than those circumstances — it stemmed from a lifetime of suffering and maybe even more than one. Growing up in a home with mental illness and addiction left me with many unresolved feelings, patterns and beliefs about the nature of life and love. I continued to repeat those patterns despite years of therapy, spiritual healing and the beginning of the recovery process. There was progress and there was still a lot of pain, too.

I love how the universe works to bring you exactly where you need to be. Needing to make ends meet while I was rebuilding my holistic healing practice in a new state, I decided to take on a part-time job. It happened to be with a woman who ran her own school of spiritual healing. I worked for her for just a short time to help her get her own business going as she had recently relocated as well. The synergy of our backgrounds and experiences was a great support for me during that time.

When her new program, University Of The Heart, began the next year in Maryland, I had the opportunity to attend. Although I had helped with the business development and marketing of this program, I really didn't know what exactly to expect from this year-long intensive program. I knew I needed to make some changes in my life. Even with my work beginning to come together, I found myself stuck in the grief process and trapped in what I was just beginning to recognize as an unhealthy and abusive relationship. I needed something to help move me forward in my life, so when the opportunity came, I went for it.

I would say that at that point in 2003, having already spent a good part of my life focused on holistic and spiritual healing, I considered myself somewhat well versed in heart-centered living. What I learned that year was that I basically needed to throw the manual I had received for this lifetime out the window and create a new "book of life" for myself. I came to see that what I believed about love and life was very distorted and that this was not just in my own experience, but from a collective one as well.

As I alluded to earlier, one of the big things that I began to uncover that year was that many of my feelings and beliefs around love and life were distorted. I came to understand the blueprint my heart was holding as truth at that time and I began to see how this misperception was affecting my life on many levels. Here are some of the beliefs I discovered that I was holding about love at that time:

Love is unsafe.
Love is dangerous.
Love is unstable and unpredictable.
Love is explosive.
Love is hurtful.
Love is conflict.
Love is abuse.
Love is denying my true self to please, satisfy and care for others.
Love is sacrifice.
Love is giving my power away.
Love is manipulative.
Love is pain.
Love is scary.
Love is unsafe.
Love requires pain.
I am undeserving of love.

A big part of the process that year was to uncover these limiting feelings, patterns and beliefs, to release them and to begin to build a new paradigm for love in my life. As part of our group process, we focused on our individual experiences as well as supporting the collective in transforming these patterns. Seeing this list now, I wonder how I ever related with anyone in an intimate and loving way. And yet, all of this was right there inside of me, driving and directing my relationships, experiences and life choices.

Another aspect of the journey was to access my soul purpose on a deeper level, from a place of the true heart, not one of misperception. This again involved uncovering distortions and really allowing my true voice to emerge as a guiding force in my life. I learned that in order to access heart wisdom I need to be committed, consistent and willing to slow down, be still and invite in a deeper and authentic relationship with myself to emerge.

At the end of that year, I was asked to write an essay on the following questions:

"What are the major pieces that I've learned this year about my heart that will help me to choose a more loving future for myself?"

"What does assuming responsibility have to do with it?"

Here are the answers that I wrote at that time:

"I've learned that it's okay to love myself. It's not selfish to love myself - it's actually generous because by learning to love myself, I increase my ability to love others and bring more love into the world. Loving myself is an act of service that is essential to my own evolution, to that of creation and to the fulfillment of my soul mission.

I've also learned that I deserve love - not because of what I do, how I act, how much money I make or whom I please, but because it is my birthright as a being, as a part of the divine love continuum. I deserve love because I am love. And, to deprive myself of that is a denial of my own true self.

I've learned that there are certain essentials for the heart, which will allow me to create true love - love without pain and suffering, love that can be trusted, and love that is nurturing and fulfilling.

These essentials offer the foundational basis for choosing to live a loving life. They include:

- Going slow
- Consistency
- Listening to my heart
- Allowing my feelings
- Time and attention
- Gentleness
- Being open and honest with myself
- Following the calling of my soul
- Nurturing myself and my heart
- Being in alignment with my self and source
- Taking care of myself on all levels — physically, mentally, emotionally and spiritually
- Building trust with my self and others
- Maintaining awareness of who I truly am, of my connection to source and of being multidimensional
- Not overriding my feelings because of logic or someone else's agenda
- Staying true to my heart no matter what!

Above all, I've learned that I am a heart being. And, that by staying centered in that truth and taking the time to honor it, I can be my true self without doubt and confusion. All of life's answers lie within my heart and soul. Fulfillment comes from knowing and being in alignment with my self and God, not from any other person or thing.

Assuming responsibility for my life and my heart supports me in choosing a more loving life. It allows me to create the life, work, and relationships, which my true heart desires. It takes me out of victimhood and into my power, where I can create a new blueprint for my heart and for living love.

I can choose to let go of all of the energies, which no longer serve me; and I can bring in the energies, which support my growth and evolution. I have the power within me, by aligning my heart with Source.

By accepting responsibility, I am able to respond to the needs of my heart and to the directive of my soul, for my own highest good, that of the universe and all creation. This is the path to a more loving future and by choosing to create a more loving future, I move more and more into love each and every day."

Having taken this year-long journey devoted to Love and the path of the heart, I know what dedication, willingness and courage it took for the women of Tender Voices: True Stories By Women On A Journey Of Love to walk this path together over the last year. Each Heal My Voice book offers an opportunity not just to write a story but also to delve deeply into an aspect of life and to search for understanding, healing and awakening. This book that you hold in your hands is a BOOK OF LOVE and represents a journey into the heart of these 16 amazing women.

I hope these stories inspire you to take your own journey into the heart, to explore what Love means to you and to begin to create a new paradigm for your life.

Many blessings on your journey!

Beth Terrence's vision is to support others in living a heart-centered, balanced and joyful life through discovering the healer within. She is a Shaman, Holistic Health & Wellness Practitioner, Speaker, Writer and Recovery Coach. She believes that her own life journey has served as a catalyst for the message she brings to the world – that at our core, we are all beings of love, light and peace – we just need to "remember". In addition to being a Heal My Voice author, Beth is also a facilitator of a pilot HMV project, which brings writing, creativity and holistic resources to women in long-term addictions treatment and recovery. She resides in Annapolis, MD, with her loving partner, Mario and her cats, Mossimo and Clover. Visit Beth's website at www.bethterrence.com.

Editor's Note

Andrea Hylen

Founder of Heal My Voice

As this book is coming to a close, I have been staying with a friend of mine in Baltimore where I am surrounded by love in action.

Kate is a teacher who is committed to teaching and supporting her students at the elementary and college level. She is a mother who is dedicated to her children and is modeling love for her daughter and son in the choices and decisions she makes with her time, money, energy and boundaries. Her daughter, Molly is a 10th grade high school student.

During this last week, Molly has been going to a summer camp as a counselor where every day is filled with love and service and fun. The teenagers have packed lunches and picked produce for people experiencing homelessness. Today they are going to a nursing home in the city to spend time with a poor, elderly population of men and women. More than the activities, I am aware of how Molly is going into the world everyday to spread love. Her heart is open wide. Her eyes are bright. She is spreading love with a community to another community. Everyone is happier and generating even more love. That is what love in action does.

Last month I was in New York with a group of actors who had just returned from three weeks in Ecuador with Dramatic Adventure Theatre. Through the experiences of living in villages, observing and participating, the actors returned feeling connected, inspired and transformed as they wrote and performed plays woven with love.

In a few days, I am headed to Sweden and I will be teaching at an event called The Joyride Malmo: Love in Action. The event was created after a desire to bring people together in joy, love and connection.

What's love got to do with it? Everything!

*Love is an open door…*that just keeps opening more.

Both of those lines are from songs that talk about the heartbreak and opening that comes from loving. So, which do you choose? The women in this book have opened their hearts to look at love in their lives. The love of a parent, a child, a partner, God and a love journey that, in the writing, has led all of them to more self-love and willingness to love again. They have written about heartache and joy and a myriad of emotions where they remembered a journey of love.

I want to thank all of the women who wrote stories in this book. They had the courage to dive into vulnerable, raw spots in their lives that were happening at the same time they were writing. Each of them courageously showed you how to keep your heart open and what we can all learn from love.

Thank you to Liz Draman for agreeing to co-facilitate this project with me. I learned so much in our collaboration. She is a love warrior with a mission of love. The love she shares with her daughter and partner in love, Alan, is a road map for us all.

I have been transformed by the stories in this book and I am grateful. I encourage you to read the stories with an open heart and know that by allowing yourself to feel all of the feelings, they will open your heart even wider. Surrender to the love.

In love and gratitude and peace within, Andrea

Andrea Hylen believes in the power of a woman's voice to usher in a new world. She is the founder of Heal My Voice, a Minister of Spiritual Peacemaking, a Desire Based Coach and Orgasmic Meditation teacher. Andrea has discovered her unique gifts while parenting three daughters and learning to live life fully after the deaths of her brother, son and husband. She is currently living out of a suitcase following her intuition as she collaborates with women and men in organizations and travels around the world speaking, teaching and leading workshops. Her passion is authentically living life and supporting others in doing the same. To connect with Andrea and learn about current projects go to: www.andreahylen.com and www.healmyvoice.org.

Introduction

Liz Draman

When I met Andrea Hylen in 2009 *Heal My Voice* was in its gestation period. Our meeting at a Silver Violet Flame class she gave with Jayne Howard Feldman at Breathe Books in Baltimore, MD was a reunion of two women who remembered a soul agreement to walk a path of Love. That can be said for all of the women who come together in the *Heal My Voice* book circles. We come together to remember – who we are, what we came here to do, and to reclaim the pieces of our heart fragmented along the pathway of life. It does not matter what road we travel they all lead us back to Love.

In Andrea's style of complete and utter trust, in May of 2011 at an inner city church in Baltimore Maryland the first *Heal My Voice* fundraiser emerged on a wing and prayer. Andrea has a way of rallying her tribe in true Girl Scout leader style; she ignites a sister and brotherhood that draws out the generosity in people. I was happy to dive in to support her along with my sweetheart, Love Troubadour Alan Peterson. Alan's song *In Any Given Moment* inspired Andrea in 2008 to take a leap of faith and follow the Jonas Brother band on a cross country tour with her daughter Hannah. The three of us became good friends as we shared the breakdowns and breakthroughs that come with growing into who you truly are.

When the first book circle formed there was no question, I was in. Writing my story in *Fearless Voices* in 2011 was my next evolutionary step. In a circle of 20 powerful healers, priestesses, successful business women, mom's and seasoned writers I began to heal my relationship with women. In their honest loving reflections I recognized the many masks I wore to protect my tender heart. A source of creative expression was awakened in me. There was more to discover about myself so I signed on for *Inspired Voices* in 2012. As life reflected the metamorphoses I was undergoing I found comfort in our weekly community calls and private facebook group. Coming to our calls honoring whatever was up for each woman without needing to fix each other, allowed Love to do what love does – heal.

During *Inspired Voices* Andrea and I began having private conversations about love. Like researchers learning more about who we are as women, we explored our feelings openly; nothing was off limits. As we shared our experiences of searching for a deeper connection of intimacy with ourselves and in relationships we thought: *Let's invite others into our conversation.* Let's do a radio show! And the *Voices of Love* blogtalk radio show was conceived. I was somewhat new to radio shows and supporting me in taking my big next step in being "seen" in my Brilliance – my biggest fear - is just one way Andrea rallies her authors to show up.

But there was more.

It didn't occur to us what was forming from our pure joy of our co-creation, a new book circle. One Sunday morning I had the inspiration that we were being called to co-facilitate a book project *Voices of Love.* The bigger vision was *Voices of*

Love would someday include women as well as men. As we hold the vision for potential future book projects that will include our brothers we are remembering what it truly means to love ourself.

In January 2013, we opened the doors for the fourth Heal My Voice book circle. Two other book projects were getting under way simultaneously *Voices of Peace* and *Voices of Feminine Leadership*. Love, Peace and Feminine Leadership are not small topics to delve into. The coming year would surely be one of great expansion for everyone involved.

As our Voices of Love circle formed at first with a burst of creative juice Andrea and I were unaware of the detour not far ahead. Reflecting on the past year we now see, to hold the space for the profound inner work the women of our group would meet, we as facilitators were called to go deeper in our own transformation like never before. In May of 2014 Andrea and I reached a crossroad, our paths lead us in different directions for a time to complete the next step of our journey. The women of our group were in their parallel process, each living out our story.

This dynamic showed up as women came in to the group with a big presence then faded to the background, others joined ready to write their story of love to realize they resonated more with one of the other book circles. As we rode the waves of our evolving stories, trusting the process, our circle coalesced and strengthened with each shift. Over the months as we each opened fully to our stories we began to touch the energy of self-compassion. One morning I received an email from Andrea who shared excitedly she woke with the book's new and very apropos title – Tender Voices: True Stories by Women on a Journey of Love.

I believe we are the priceless sum of what we came to our planet as – LOVE - and all of the experiences we've accumulated in our life journey. It is in the sharing our experiences that satisfies our deep yearning for connection. In the healing stories shared in Tender Voices, you will remember part of you asking to be loved. Remember to breathe, for breath moves energy and opens the door for Love and Compassion to dissolve the wall of protection around your heart. As you share our journey to love allow yourself to feel and touch the power in our vulnerability. As we awaken Love in our stories, Love awakens in you and our world.

Our world is demanding love to awaken. Not the kind of love that makes sense to our logical mind, rather new stage in human evolution "heart thinking"; the kind of love that heals, brings resolution and creates. It is the kind of love that "hate" surrenders to and restores peace and harmony in our world.

How can we experience this kind of love? The stories in this book are your sacred guides; each voice uniquely expressing a transparency, courage, and vulnerability with the raw honesty that will liberate the healing Power of Love in you.

Thank you for sharing our journey to Love.

Liz Draman *was inspired to create her vision, Awaken to Love as a movement toward living from the heart of who you are ~ illuminating a path to your inner brilliance and conscious living. She is a passionate awakener of Conscious Love, Light and Life and an active teacher committed to spiritual education and empowering women to awaken their Divine-Power. www.lizdraman.com*

Liz is dedicated to walking this scared path in own life and for the past 24 years has shared the journey with the joy of her life, her daughter Jillian.

Part One

I Am Compassionate

Whether we have it all or we have nothing, we are all faced with the same obstacles: sadness, loss, illness, dying and death. If we are to strive as human beings to gain more wisdom, more kindness and more compassion, we must have the intention to grow as a lotus and open each petal one by one. "

-Goldie Hawn

Story One

Life After Love

Lorie Paul

"Love is the bridge between you and everything." ~Rumi

I let go.
I forgive.
I surrender.

Bringing more love and compassion into my life.

Each day is a new beginning. A new opportunity to recreate what I love and what I want to see manifest in my life.

I Am the Captain navigating my ship.

*****

I didn't always know this. When I ended my last relationship. I had a choice to sink or swim. If you are in the same place I was with all kinds of feelings of sadness and loss and pain, I want you to know that my story, just like all the other stories in this book, is about hope and the next steps.

I want you to know that there is a light at the end of the tunnel, and there is support for you, and everything is going to be better than just ok, even if you can't see it yet.

On the other end of fear, there is love. And what you will learn is that love was there all along the way.

*****

I couldn't go on any longer doing what I had always done. I had a choice to make and only I could make it.
This choice was about retraining my brain, breaking barriers and moving out of my comfort zone, and reprogramming what I had learned as a child and through out my life.

The first step was to really forgive myself for what I was never taught or never learned and just did not know. I learned to have compassion for myself.

The second step was to accept that no matter what happened in my life, I had a choice and now it was time to fully accept and be responsible for my choices. Through gratitude I was able to see that every one of my preconceived mistakes had a gift.

It doesn't mean it was easy. At times my healing was so challenging I didn't know if I could continue. During those moments, I made a choice to honor myself. I took a break but I never stopped asking for help and gentle, clear guidance. This wasn't a race to the finish line. This was my life. When I felt stronger and more confident and ready, I would continue.

True healing began when I stopped listening to

everyone and everything outside of myself and I started listening to what was inside of me.

I learned to trust myself and I allowed myself to be vulnerable to do new things in spite of the voice in my mind saying, "This isn't how we do it." I was retraining my brain, and that's when things really started to shift for me.

*****

"We are all just walking each other home." Ram Dass

Sometimes the only thing I needed to do was to clear my path, move forward and become aware of the gifts that were being presented. I received emails with tools and I was guided to stories and books with the healing steps I needed at that time. Through all of this, I discovered how to break patterns that were keeping me in a state of fear, patterns that were keeping me small. I discovered how to open doors that were sealed shut for many years. I tapped into a place of love and joy that I didn't know existed and this newfound joy had a rippling effect on others.

When I changed, everything around me changed. My relationships were taken to a new level of love and respect, my finances shifted, and the extra pounds that I put on began to melt away. I felt peace.

As I began to shift and heal, my soul kept bringing up more and more old beliefs and hurts that were ready to be released for healing. Many times this was very scary. Keeping my faith and trusting that Spirit is always assisting me with divine healing brought me great peace. Keeping my heart open and knowing I will always be guided. I learned to trust that feeling in my body.

I began asking for my truth.

When I decided to put my old story behind me and began writing my new story that was the turning point. The story of the new me, my higher agreements with myself, and my hearts desires. I decided to go BIG this time. No matter how crazy or big my new desires seemed to me, I was going for them and I began saying them out loud and claiming them.

I wrote my new story, the story of how I want my life to be right now. It doesn't have to all happen at once. I know it will come in Divine time. It will come when I am ready for it, and I will keep growing to prepare for what change is needed so I can receive it..

I read my new story every night before bed and I let the story play out in my mind. Before I begin reading, I set the tone. I light a candle. I bring in love and light and blessings and most of all gratitude. I make sure that I am filled with love in my heart. As I begin to read, I see my story come to life. I imagine myself there already. I hear voices. I see details. I notice scents. I notice how I feel. I notice how I look and who I'm with. I go to the deepest part of my imagination and I activate the deepest form of gratitude and appreciation for what I desire. I feel as if I am already there and I already have it. I also speak like it is already mine. The words I choose are very powerful and each word carries a vibration. I choose my words wisely.

Another healing tool is a vision board. I created a vision board to activate pictures in my mind. I have it hanging in my bedroom where I can see it everyday and I give thanks for already receiving everything on it even if I haven't yet, because I know it's coming.

It took me many years to create a vision board. I was afraid to actually let someone see my hopes and dreams or to let anyone know that much about me. I am no longer afraid.

With this deep feeling of love, my new story, the real story of me has to emerge. The magic has started to happen.

Here are some more tips:

I wake up 15 minutes earlier than I have to everyday, and I start listing everything that I am grateful for and why I am grateful. I do this before I get out of bed. Then, I give thanks for the things I would like to accomplish today. As I speak it, I feel as if it is already done. In my mind, I see the end result, as I want it. "This or something better...and so it is!"

I journal before I go to bed. It helps me reflect on my thoughts and my day, and it's a way of working out my daily stuff instead of keeping it inside. I let my thoughts flow no matter what comes up. I am careful that I don't get caught up in negative emotions. I always guide myself towards a positive outcome knowing that there is a solution for every problem.

I practice some sort of spirituality daily to keep myself grounded and present. Violet Flame decrees have proven to be the most powerful decrees that I have ever used. I say them in the morning, during the day and at night.

I have found that with my spirituality, when I skip a day or days, because I think my life is going so well, I start to lose faith, and I really start to spiral downward. I love and honor myself way too much now to let that slip away from me. I come first now and that makes for a happier, healthier, fun, loving and confident me.

Things I have learned:

That my self-talk is most important. I quiet my mind long

enough to pretend that I am talking to my best friend, what would I say and how would I speak?

I know I choose to see the best in all of my friends, so why wouldn't I see the best in me. I know if my best friend was sad or upset, I would speak to them with kindness, compassion, love, understanding, patience and tenderness so, why in the world would I speak to myself differently?

I stay strong and I don't let a bad experience or bad day ruin all that I have worked for, I keep reaching for relief. I rise above the situation and look down on it like it's so small in the big picture of my life. I have faith; I trust in what I cannot see but what I feel in my heart.

For me knowing and accepting that I Am always in the right place, with the right people, at the right time, doing the right thing always brings a great sense of peace to my life. I trust in the process of my journey, and I have faith that I Am always being guided towards whatever is in my highest good and I accept that all is well now.

I find that I give to everyone and I neglect my own needs too often. Sometimes I use others as a form of distraction so I don't have to deal with my own problems. I now choose to clear my path of clutter and distractions and devote time to serving me. This is the highest form of honor I could ever give to myself and to the world.

I have spent the last few years empowering myself and that impacts the women around me and the women I connect with and that is my purpose. I've always had a passion for helping women to become empowered because I know that when you Empower a Woman, You Empower her family, and when you Empower her Family, you Empower her Community, and When you Empower her Community, you Empower Women all over the World... because deep down women love sharing what they have learned and they love sharing their joys with other women, it's just our nature, and it's one of the most endearing qualities in a woman. It's how we bond. If you don't have a support group of women, find them now!

And now here are the higher truths that are the power for my new story:

My higher truths...

I Am honest and I speak with honor; therefore; I am always honored.

I honor my truth; therefore; I Am authentic.

I give with love; therefore; I receive with love.

I receive with love; therefore; I Am filled with gratitude.

I honor my body; therefore; it honors me.

I Am generous; therefore; my life is full of abundance.

I am cheering you on to write your new story and to begin creating your magical journey and thank you for being a part of mine.

Lorie Paul *is a passionate writer, speaker and healer. A divorced mom of three children and a few relationships under her belt, she knows what it's like to experience both true love and loss. Lorie understands the beautiful gifts each relationship has brought into her life. A true advocate for empowering women to find the courage to conquer their fears. If you would like to contact her for tips, tools, advice or to share your story of courage and healing email her at loriepaulLove@gmail.com or follow her page on Facebook*

Story Two

Who Stole My Voice?

Deborah E. Niver

Who among us has had her voice yanked out from under her and may or may not have realized it? Mine was "stolen" in a previous lifetime. Why, how, where, and from whom, I do not know. I just know it happened. I looked up the word steal and it means "to take away by force or unjust means or to take without permission." *WOW--I felt like I was hit by a bolt of lightning!!*

First Words

I did not start speaking until I was three years old. I remember my Mom telling me that she and my Dad took me to several doctors to make sure I was healthy and were told, "She just is not ready to talk."

Mom says once I started talking, I did not stop—which was true around people I knew well. Being a very shy person, I seldom spoke unless I was spoken to. Although I finally found my voice at three years of age, it has been "stolen" since then on more than one occasion in this lifetime. When I do speak, many people do not hear what I have to say. It is as if I am speaking in a foreign language or talking to a wall.

I have always had trouble speaking my Truth. I would sit back and observe everything happening around me but seldom spoke up. The first time I had a spiritual reading, I asked, "Why am I afraid to speak my Truth especially about my spirituality?" He replied, "You were punished in a previous lifetime for speaking up but you are safe in this lifetime."

Unfortunately, I still do not speak my Truth about many important topics and I needed to know why. It is the reason I signed up for "Voices of Love" to find out who stole my voice and how to get it back.

The Sound of My Voice

The first time I can remember my voice being yanked from me was in first or second grade. Our class was singing and the young girl next to me told me: "to sit down and shut up—I was knocking her off tune." I was absolutely humiliated. I could feel myself turn red in the face. After that incident, I would mouth words but would not sing aloud except at home. At home, we were all off tune so it did not matter. Just as important, I started to become self-conscious of the sound of my voice.

In 8th grade, my music teacher wanted us to sing even if we were off tune; we were to sing from our heart. I was very self-conscious singing aloud so I sang "quietly aloud" from my heart. I still never sing around strangers or with someone who has a wonderful voice.

I was in second or third grade when the school contacted my parents and said I had a lisp. I could not pronounce the "s" sound—a common lisp issue. I took speech classes to learn how to enunciate words correctly. You are required to exaggerate your lips and tongue movements as you learn to enunciate different sounds. The speech pathologist recorded my voice so I could hear my lisp as well as the correct enunciation of the words. Just to let you know, your voice sounds different to your own ears than to others' ears. Again, I was really embarrassed and hated the sound of my voice on the recorder. It took me over a year to get rid of the lisp. I don't remember other children making fun of my lisp; yet, as I learned to enunciate words correctly they would make fun of me because I spoke slowly and clearly. After all that work, I quickly learned to use slang or drop the "ing" off of words. A good example is I am "goin" to the store. This habit has continued as an adult, and it still makes me self-conscious.

The Meaning of Words

I was in fourth grade with a teacher who believed if you were not an "A" student you were stupid. And she told you so! This began my negative feelings towards authority. She wanted to hold back the entire class. My Mom asked how I felt about this and I replied if I needed to stay back I guess I would. Since she didn't want to see me struggle in school, she kept me back that year. In hindsight, I really did not understand the ramifications of being kept behind. Staying back a year, made me think and feel that I was stupid. This has truly affected my confidence throughout my life especially when taking on a new course of study.

I honestly do not remember her asking me how I felt. I was an adult by the time I asked my Mom why she held me back, and she replied she had asked for my opinion at the time. I am blessed that I had a Mom who was concerned about my feelings and wanted my input on something that important; I was also angry that my Mom would even listen to such a teacher.

The second time around in fourth grade, I had a female teacher who wanted me to feel "special." I was responsible for taking a note to the principal's office about a male classmate who kept getting in trouble. He had problems at home—his parents were going through personal issues which affected him. I was uncomfortable and miserable handling such a mission and began to dislike both the teacher and the principal. The principal would bring a paddle to the classroom, humiliate the child by reprimanding him in front of his classmates, and then spank him in front of everyone. I really felt sorry for him. I remember looking at him one day and we made eye contact. I remember es"specially" hating myself for taking the note to the principal's office and believing my classmate hated me. Finally I told my Mom what was happening and she had the teacher quit assigning me the task of taking the note to the principal's office. This experience traumatized me and I have struggled to forgive myself because of the impact those incidents had on my classmate. I would like to contact him and let him know how I felt. It had a pronounced affect on my relationships with authority.

When I was a teenager, my Mom once told me to look up words to be sure I knew the definition of them prior to using them in a sentence. She explained that I had used the wrong words on a couple of occasions. Fortunately, she told me when we were alone. I was still embarrassed that I had used the wrong words and it is just one more thing that makes me self-conscious and afraid to speak.

Afraid to Use my Voice

In the area that I grew up, there was only one church of my ethnic background that everyone attended. My Mom would tell us to watch what we said because everyone was related to someone else. As a child, I did not know anything personal about the people in church to tell anyone. What could I possibly say? Since I was afraid that I would say the wrong thing I never spoke to anyone. When I was asked questions, I would give a "yes/no" answer or "I don't know."

Even as an adult, after asking me a question, people have actually walked away from me in the middle of my answer. How humiliating is that!! I do not know if I am boring, if it is a lack of interest in what I am saying, or if it is their personal issue. No matter the reason, it hurts and it is embarrassing.

These are only a few of the incidences that have occurred in my life. As I have told these stories to others, I never felt there were major repercussions other than my being embarrassed. That is so far from the Truth. I have subconsciously been carrying within my heart hurt, anger, and resentment. All these experiences have impacted my confidence and interactions with others.

How many times can a person be told to be quiet, you are stupid, give me the bottom line, or have someone walk away in the middle of a conversation before you go crawling back into your own shell? I often think, "What could I possibly say that is worth someone's time to listen to me?"

I find myself speaking quickly and leaving out pertinent information fearing the other person will cut me off from the conversation. In doing so, it leaves way too much room for miscommunication. This has caused many issues in my relationships. Even on answering machines I blurt out messages in fear that the person receiving the message will hang up without listening to my comments; therefore, my conversations do not always flow well.

Healing My Voice

As I began journaling my story and looking back on how these experiences have affected me throughout my life, I was sad and had a lot of anger within. Often my mind literally closes down in fear when directly asked a question from an instructor, or asked to pray aloud, or to spontaneously speak. No wonder that I have struggled learning new subjects, panic over taking tests, and feel very insecure in classes. It goes well beyond that. It has affected my creativity, decision-making, forming opinions about major topics and world events, or speaking these opinions aloud because others may not agree with me.

I had lots of anger to work through with myself and with people who had misused their authority. I was angry with myself that I had allowed others to steal my voice, thus stealing my power, and convincing me that I was stupid.

Andrea, the Founder of Heal My Voice, recorded the first draft of this story, reading it out loud so I could "hear my voice." I cried when she told me what she had done. I was nervous about listening to the story because it would make everything real. It would no longer be held just in my head and heart. I was truly blessed when I heard it read back to me; a great healing took place. I was able to see the story from a different angle.

I had to look within to determine: Why was I willing to let others steal my voice and basically give away my power? What changes did I need to make within so I no longer repeated these experiences? It's similar to the movie Ground Hog Day. The character lived the same day over and over until he learned his lesson. Now that I saw this, what would it take to reclaim my voice and to empower myself?

Everything is Energy

We are all One and interconnected with all living beings in the Universe. What we see in others is a reflection of ourselves. As a daughter, aunt, sister, supervisor, wife, friend or whatever, I wonder, whose voice have I unknowingly stolen when I was training, coaching, advising, or just talking to someone?

As I look back over these experiences, I don't think any of the people involved in these incidences were being purposefully mean. I think they were doing the best that they knew how to do under the circumstances. Just as I need to let go of resentment, forgive others, and grow from these experiences, I also need to take responsibility for my own actions. I need to forgive myself for giving away my power by letting others steal my voice as well as for what I may have done to others.

Through my spiritual growth and healing work, I have learned that everything is energy. Energy is a vibration and we are created in the energy of love. There are seven major energy fields known as chakras located along our spinal cord. Our vocal cords are located in our throat chakra also known as the power chakra—the one we use to speak with authority.

It affects our creativity and our self- expression. It is a crossover between the physical and spiritual worlds. It represents our search for Truth, recognizing the "I AM" within each of us, and owning one's power. Love should always be flowing in and through us as we co-create our lives and the world around us through our thoughts, words, and actions. I find this fascinating since I have struggled speaking my Truth regarding my spirituality and that I was willing to give up my own power. It is amazing how our body, mind, and spirit work together.

I Have a Voice

I recently took a class at the Strathmore Hall Foundation, Inc. entitled, "So you think you can't sing?" I was terrified and excited too. The teacher was alive with music and he lived it through his heart and expressed it in all aspects of his life. He taught with humor and was lots of fun. He invited each of us to work individually with him prior to class. We would sing while he played the piano as he listened to where our pitch matched the musical scale. That was scary in itself. Many other classmates also came early so they could work with him. That meant we would hear each other sing. It took a lot of courage but I was determined. You know what?? --- I can sing—an entire octave!! I have no desire to join a choir but when I hear a song on the radio, I sing aloud. Is that cool or what!!

As I breathe in the breath of God, I let go of my fears and allow love to express through me fully. This story has been a gift in itself. I am living in gratitude for all those who have come to be a part of my life's journey teaching me to own my authority, to honor and respect the love and compassion I have for others by expressing it fully, and to forgive myself and others. Since writing this story, I am a different person.

I am gradually reclaiming my personal power in the Universe. From now on, I am singing in all aspects of my life. As I empower myself, it will be to my tune, to my Truth, and to my own special vibrational frequency that connects me with the Divine. Her love and wisdom that lives in me will be expressed through me in my thoughts, words, and actions.

It will be expressed with my Voice.

Deborah E. Niver Her greatest passion is helping others to heal themselves. While on her own spiritual journey she realized we are all connected to Universal energy and our every thought, feeling, word, and deed creates a ripple in the Universe the same way a stone hitting the water creates a ripple in the entire pond. This led her to become a Licensed Unity Teacher, Licensed Massage Therapist, and Healing Touch Practitioner for Animals and Healing Touch Practitioner Associate for people. She lives at home with her husband, David, and their two dogs Jasper and Sophie, and their cat Jake.

Story Three

Ensouling Words:
Remembering the Sacred Scribe Within

Amber Lee Scott

Despite the cold, my legs carried me like an agile cat across the blustery campus. Breathing deeply, heart pumping in anticipation of the wondrous words I was sure awaited me. Even the wind whipping my face and tunneling deep into my ears was no match for my steam engine. Throwing wide the doors, I entered. Body warm, yet cool and damp from the sweat, I flew up the antiquated staircase to the door of my destiny.

Inside my English Professor's office, I found an envelope with the name "Amber" written in red. I ripped it open, only to find a barrage of blood stained ink across every page. My poem, my heart, lay lacerated in my own small stubby hands. *"Are you sure you want to publish this poem? Once published, you can never take it back. If you still proceed, I invite you to rewrite it with my corrections."* These wounding words tunneled through my veins. Each line given the harsh penetrating neon light of examination.

The blow shattered me into little pieces. Instead of picking up the pieces and gluing them back together with love, confidence, and trust, I chose to put down the pen. I chose to let the words of another decide the direction of my life. I dimmed my light, closed my heart, and agreed I wasn't enough - good enough, smart enough, pretty enough, funny enough. At that moment, I folded my soft delicate petals and hid my beauty from the world. The Sacred Scribe lost her way and wandered many years in the desert before uncovering her passion once again.

Forgetting who I AM became a pattern, like a quilt of experiences sewn together and locked deep in the heart chest. The key was long lost, misplaced, forgotten. Even now, I thumb through my parents' yellowed picture albums with awe and a little trepidation. Trying to remember. Piecing together the stories my parents tell and these faded snapshots of a childhood gone by.

Remember

Memories
Memories
Hazy and grey
Memories
Memories
Beg me to stay
Memories
Memories
Of love most dear
Memories
Memories
Nothing to fear

Although fuzzy, I remember moments of full expression. Dancing around my house on tiptoes to the enchanting rhythms of the Nutcracker. I was a ballerina, an ordinary child turned into a princess after a battle with the Mouse King. Dance and music have always lived in my soul.

Born in the late seventies, I grew up listening to Led Zeppelin, Jimi Hendrix, The Beatles White Album, and The Talking Heads. I sang at the top of my lungs, to the audience in my imagination. I brought joy, understanding, and unity to my imaginary friends and myself through my unadulterated expression.

Ballet classes, cheerleading, church choir, and bell choir were all short-lived experiences, never bringing me the joy I found in dancing and singing with pure abandon in the comfort of my own home and from my own soul. I feel most free in expression when there is no one to critique and no one to tell me the "right" way to BE.

I AM that I AM

I forgot the Coulds
Held fast to the Shoulds
All the voices so clear
Except the ONE most near
The fog so thick
Clock goes tick, tick, tick
Lost out at sea
Who is the real me?
Feels like a lie
So…
Who am I?

My love for words and poetry blossomed in high school. I smile, remembering the many joy-filled hours I invested in birthing poems at "The Art Works." My art store gig became a place of refuge and often solitude. The art-lined walls inspired and called to me, filling the room with creativity. In these moments, I became living breathing art. My soul poured onto the page, ensouling each word with feeling, emotion, and the rhythm of my heart.

As an empath, writing gave me an outlet to express, release, and move the emotion and energy that flowed through my body and mind. For me, the written word contained codes and secret messages from my heart and soul. As a Sacred Scribe, I AM a pure vessel for Divine Love and Light to flow through me and onto the page. Each ensouled word brings new awareness and new meaning to my life's purpose, my gifts, and my heart's desire.

I believe we are ALL art. To be on eARTh, is to be art. In my experience, art is co-creation and self-expression from the heart and soul. I forgot this truth, denying myself freedom through self-expression for most of my twenties.

The climax of my severance from my heart and soul manifested itself into a stale cookie cutter career as a Senior Cost Analyst for a 75 million dollar government contract. Slave to the traffic lights, fluorescent lights, and my dimly-lit computer screen, my soul began to suffer.

Until one day, when a VERY special creation came my way. A little, baby girl, so sweet. How can there be any art more hallowed than the joining together of male and female in love and sacred ceremony? The growing child within, fused to my being, listening to the music of my heart, reminded me of possibility, magic and mystery.

All art has a gestation period. You are pregnant with possibility and then a final push and birthing of your co-creation comes forth into the world. To me, ensouling words is much like this process. A birthing of the word made flesh.

Like a caterpillar who emerged from the chrysalis, my life was forever changed. Being a mother gave me new eyes to see and new ears to hear. During pregnancy, I experienced heightened senses like nothing I have ever encountered. I could smell, taste and touch with almost superhuman powers. In my experience, pregnancy and motherhood was truly a spiritual awakening and a remembering of who I AM.

As I grew to see myself reflected in my daughter, I began to love and appreciate myself again. To take special care of her, I had to first take special care of me. To teach her, I had to become the teaching. To become the teaching, I had to listen to and express my TRUTH.

Realize with Real Eyes

I (k)**NOW** have eyes to see
I (k)**NOW** have ears to hear
The love and light inside
I hold most dear
We are the truth, the light and the way
Whether at work, home, or play
We live in God and (s)he in us
We ride together in the big blue and green bus

One way I was guided back to the full expression of my truth was in the creation of my first blog. By birthing a blog, the sacred art of writing returned to me. " A Life in Balance - Project Do What You Love" became a catalyst for helping me find balance and come back to center. My proclamation to find the courage to follow my heart echoed through the world wide web. I AM seen. I AM heard. I AM speaking my truth. I AM facing my fears. I AM doing what I love, in love and by love.

My desire quickly manifested into a burning fire to spend more time with my daughter and create a livelihood from writing. A year after her birth, my corporate climbing days were over. Taking a huge leap of faith and trust that God and the Universe always provide for all my earthly needs, True U Voice was born. Today, I facilitate a connection of heart & soul by creating a safe and sacred space for my clients' messages to emerge. I am honored to witness so many people stepping up to their calling, giving their gifts, and living their passions. These courageous souls are assisting the planet and becoming visible in a whole new way through the world wide web.

I believe the organic expression of who we ARE becomes intimately connected to our happiness and our aliveness. Our gifts and talents are intermingled with our life's purpose. Without purpose, we often feel like a wanderer on a dark highway. Purpose shines a light and directs us to a path of joy, service, and the feeling of being needed, accepted, and loved.

By writing and publishing this story, I continue to move forward fearlessly, igniting courage, breaking through barriers and plowing my blockages to expand beyond my limitations into joy and freedom. I continue to listen to my own inner knowing and true voice, the voice of my soul. I NOW enjoy (in joy) many types of self-expression including sacred drumming, photography, and even the occasional painting or drawing. And yes, I still dance around my house singing at the top of my lungs. If you see me getting down in my car, I hope it brings a smile to your face and a realization that you too are FREE to express the musings of your soul.

I AM enough.
I AM made in the image and likeness of a Divine Creator and a loving God.
I remember who I AM.
I choose to serve with my gifts.
I give and receive in full love.
I trust in Spirit and Divine Guidance.
I AM a unique expression of the Divine.
I AM safe to live in FULL expression of my soul, my creativity, my joy, and my love.
I feel words.
I ensoul words.
I speak my truth.
I speak love.

God is LOVE.
I AM love.
You are love.
When we all remember this as our true essence, we walk everyday in the Promised Land.
It dwells within us, not without us.

Amber Lee Scott's True U Voice *is an extension of her enthusiasm for holistic healing, giving back to Mother Earth, raising the vibration of our planet, and the true power of LOVE and God.*

With a B.S. in Environmental Science, Amber knows the importance of living a life in balance with nature. She's combines her knowledge with project management, marketing, and writing experience to heal the world, while facilitating her client's vision and values into their voice.

Amber helps her clients find balance in the new virtual era by building authentic real social media relationships, in your very own True U Voice style!
http://www.trueUvoice.com/
https://www.facebook.com/trueUvoice/

Story Four

Patterns of Life:
Consciously Living Day by Day

Nichole Shannon

Mother May I

We are patterns of life
Struggling day by day
Mother may I see the way

My hearts grown empty

Options all dead,
As I lay here abandoned
In our bed

Thought I was enough
Guess I am just a fool
Turning into the little girl
I once knew

Mamma dressed me pretty
Always combed my hair
Then picked out Daddy's
Favorite dress for me to wear

By the front door I'd wait
For daddy to show,
though he never came..
Eighteen years later same ole game

We are patterns of life
Struggling day by day
Mother may I see the way

It's quarter to three
And you'll be home...
I wake to the car and
Reach for the comb

Make sure I'm pretty
And everything's just so
Maybe one day like Daddy
You'll know

You near the bed and I see your eyes
My heart can't help what it denies
Woman or child, I learn someday
What I need to do to make you stay

We are patterns of life
Struggling day by day
Mother may I see the way
Mother help me, Break Away

Mother may I see the way…

We are just patterns of life.

My life is the same as any other life. I inhale, I exhale; just as every other living creature. It is only those brief pauses in between that make my life unique to me. Then again, after forty-one years, I have learned more about those brief moments. A ceased moment in breath has been shared, a single moment when you inhale so deeply because you know your path has completely changed forever. It feels like you need to hold your breath while diving deeply simply because you are not sure when you will come up for air or where you will be.

Abuse

We live patterns of abuse until we consciously choose to courageously and lovingly, break those patterns. Abuse doesn't scream and warn like a red light. It is not seen by most outsiders. Abuse starts slowly on the inside, more like a frightened person stranded on the side of the road. You stop to help. The abuser relinquishes all control to you in that moment. Later, much later; it is you they blame and belittle and condemn. At first, it might be as small as the tire shimmies because you couldn't put it on tight enough. Subtle blaming and correcting at first. You jump in to help more. To try to get it right. And the blame escalates over time. It eventually comes to an explosion of wrongness. Their life is ruined because the spare you helped fix came off and that's why they hit a tree...

And then it changes. For a moment, the abuser's punches, threats, words, or anger stop and the next cycle starts when they withhold any and all attention. This is the person that is broken down on the side of the road and says, "I have AAA." I don't need you at all. So, you ache for the attention even when it means you can be hurt physically again. I believed it was my job, my mission, my soul purpose to make sure they realized they did need me. What a recipe for disaster!

See life happens with us seeing just fragments, like shards of glass. Happenings seem similar by the infamous memory. All we know is how we reacted last time and that we survived. So we tend to repeat that pattern. I believe with all my being that it is within us to see not just the shards of light, but the whole glowing sphere. I believe it because I have witnessed it. Everything I was taught about love, observed of love was wrong. Ok, maybe not wrong but certainly not in it's healthiest light.

INHALE

As I tell you what happened, I bet eighty percent of you

are going to think I am crazy. Please just try and stay with me and I promise it will make sense! The accident was the best thing that had ever happened to me. I was literally in the wrong job, the wrong city, the wrong house, the wrong marriage, and lastly the wrong thinking that I had to live up to every one's expectations around me, instead of living the life I wanted to live.

There was a reason the plane was delayed.

There was a reason the car rental place did not have my reservation.

There was a reason the bank transfer didn't go through and I was 50 minutes late with no options left but to grab a cab and get to the office.

I remember wondering, "Why is everything going wrong?" Well, now I know.

I was starting to pay attention. I was starting to wake up to what was really going on in my life.

I remember as I walked out of the rental place saying to myself, "Enough is enough.." I just needed it all to stop. The tears were streaming down my face. You know that moment? When you feel like you just want a break. Stop the insanity.

Who hasn't been there right?

But here's the key. I asked for a break. I literally said to the rental agent, "Oh my god, just give me a break." Then I walked out saying again, literally, "I just need all of this to stop." Staring up at the Chicago sky, face soaked in tears I pleaded with my Nana (my Angel) to make it all go away. Not 15 minutes later it did. My cab driver didn't see the red light. We crashed into the car obeying the signal, and everything stopped.

Everything.

EXHALE

I lost everything I asked to lose. My job, the city I lived in, my house, and my marriage. Also, I lost everyone's expectations of me, including my own. During this aftermath, this moment before the next inhale, the universe had answered me. Everything I knew my life to be was gone, including my own image and self-image. My shattered physical body and face became the mirror for the shattered inner body. The person that was emerging as me seemed unrecognizable to the people who knew me best. But, I guess that happens, meaning it is normal for people who see you a certain way to find it difficult to view you differently. It is with LOVE for yourself and them that eventually the dots will be connected from who you were then, to who you are now, and to who you will become.

INHALE

What I am really trying to say is very few of us experience life changes gracefully. We usually get caught up in the everyday rut and lose sight of what we want. We are so busy doing the thousands of little things to get there instead of just taking the leap. We forget to sit in stillness and just sit in LOVE. And it's perfectly normal for us to hit our heads firmly against the proverbial wall, or to have a dramatic life event that grabs our attention so fully that we are forced to re-evaluate everything.

As you know, there is nothing lost that cannot be found if sought. (A take off from my favorite Shakespeare quote.) Bottom line is your life events, despite the initial pain, are why you are where you are now. It's why I am where I am now. The hardest part is realizing, it doesn't just stop there. We are all continuously challenged. The only good thing is that when I found self LOVE I began to embrace it more gracefully.

EXHALE

I am so honored to know each person I meet. I am thrilled that we are uniting and speaking, and I am in awe of each of your courageous paths. With all my heart I hope some of what I am writing to you helps. I am in a different position now because I have a different path. We are all right where we are meant be. Hearing my message now is the perfect timing for you. Just like you will relate to what happened to me, others will relate to what has happened to you and that will be the thing that connects you.

INHALE

My most treasured dream is that a large number of women, men, and strangers can write and speak with honesty and transparency. It is through that transparency, and the fact we are speaking from the heart that connects us and creates intimacy. It amps the LOVE! I promise, which I do not do casually, I promise you will soar and at the end there will be a room full of people who will embrace your accomplishments. No longer strangers ; a room full of people that you will have inspired. A room full of people that will want to dig down and find their way, just like you!!! I'll just say while our stories are things that happen to us. We are not our stories.

With LOVE....EXHALE....

Nichole Shannon. Nikki is a Pisces woman. She believes she has been here many times before. She is as fluid as waters around her. She Loves life, Lives to help others achieve they're desires. Firmly believing you are only as good as, what you believe and who you help. She has worked extensively with souls transitioning as a geriatric and hospice nursing assistant. Certified in Kundalini Reiki, also learning many different modalities of alternative healing. Nichole resides in Baltimore, MD, but her gypsy spirit is planning to travel remaining open to where she is guided to best fulfill her purpose for serving others.

Part Two

I AM Devoted

"I knew I loved you before I met you
I think I dreamed you into life
I knew I loved you before I met you
I have been waiting all my life"

~Savage Garden

Story Five

A Voice of Love:
An Open Letter to My Daughter

Mary K. Baxter

Dear Lucille,

I tear up just thinking about writing to you. Putting my feelings into words on a page has never come easily to me. I'm a "talker", as you'll come to find as you grow, but writing to you, this is something new and scary.

Everything about this time in my life is new and scary. You are a tiny new bundle of joy in my life. (Not so tiny, I guess, as you were born 10 pounds 2.3 ounces) Every day I think I am going to mess up, mess you up, and I think and over think every action and inaction I take or don't make. You are perfect, as every baby is, and it's up to your father and I to guide you as you grow into the person you will become.

My life hasn't been easy. My path has been laid with many bumps and jagged edges. Some times I was able to avoid this pain and heartache, and other times I was not.

There will be so many lessons you learn along the way and so many things I want to share with you. I won't be able to protect you from all the hurt, and I wouldn't want to. Pain is a part of growing up. How you respond to it makes you who you are. As I sit here and type, while you take your morning nap, there are a few lessons in my mind already. You will make your own choices, but it's my job to share my experiences with you, so that your choices, and the resulting joy or pain, will be your own.

1. **Listen to your gut and trust yourself.** You will be guided to know what's best. If you're like me you'll need to talk to someone about your choices, or maybe, like your father, you'll process things internally. Either way or both, do take the time to think about your decisions. Trust your instincts. And don't be afraid to walk away from a situation.

2. **Be kind.** Your smile already lights up a room. Don't keep that smile in a box under the bed. Say please and thank you, not because it's "nice manners", but because it is the right thing to do. Be warm and have an open heart. This doesn't mean compromising your morals, using kind words does not hurt you in any way. If someone doesn't deserve your kindness, don't be passive aggressive. Stand up for what you believe, but be dignified. An honest statement said in kindness will go a lot farther than one filled with hate.

3. **Don't say, "Hate".** I am guilty of this myself, but we can work on it together. "Hate" is a strong word, and should be reserved for things that really matter. You

don't "hate" turkey or buses or that new shirt your aunt bought you... maybe you don't like those things, but again, be kind and honest and calmly say "no thanks". Especially don't say you "hate" a person... that's not being kind.

4. **Try new things.** There is nothing that makes me sadder than a person who won't try something new. And you're a kid! Everything is new to you! Everything you try is new. Don't lose that as an adult, either. You know something I tried recently? AN EPIDURAL! And let me tell you, it was wonderful! Trust your gut and weigh your options, I am not necessarily suggesting bungie jumping... but an eggplant parmesan is probably ok.

5. **Shut up sometimes.** This is a big one that I struggle with. I like to talk, I have opinions, and I love to share them. Sometimes you need to just be quiet and listen. You will learn so much about the world. Observe. Take mental notes. Look into someone's eyes and give them your attention.

6. **Surround yourself with people who lift you up.** Whether these are friends or colleagues or significant others, everyone you encounter are people you can choose to spend time with. Even your parents. We will speak to you with kind words, listen to what you have to offer and encourage and support your decisions. Choose other people in your life who will do the same. Support is a two way street, be prepared to be their cheerleaders too. Putting others down doesn't build

you up. Don't accept that from others, and hold yourself to a higher standard as well.

7. **You don't know everything.** You don't know everything, laying here, a tiny baby in your bassinet. You won't know everything when you are able to read this at 5 or 6. You won't know everything when you're turning 30. Not even on your deathbed. The sooner you know this, the easier your life will be. Don't try to control things, especially other people. Listen to other thoughts and ideas. Read. Travel. Learn. Experiences will give you perspective, but respect other peoples ideas, because their experiences may have shown them a different way. Remember that other people don't know everything either. Knowing this will help you forgive their humanity.

8. **You are beautiful.** There is going to be a time, probably in about 13 years, when someone tries to make you feel like you are not beautiful. You may have a moment of thinking that they're right, but they're not. You are warm and kind with a big heart. You have your father's big, curious eyes and your mothers glowing smile. Your mind is open and focused and willing to expand. You are the definition of beauty. That person is human and they are not feeling good about themselves. Their words are not a true reflection of you. Ignore them and whatever you do, don't you dare believe them.

9. **Be yourself.** Sometimes in life people are made to feel bad about seemingly silly things. Maybe you like music that others don't, or wear clothes that make you

feel out of place in certain groups. You are going to explore so many different communities of people and you will most certainly find yourself feeling like an outsider at some point in your life. Be proud of who you are. Different doesn't mean bad or wrong. You are incredible. I can't wait to hear your thoughts and it will be so cool to hear when they differ from my own. Other people you meet will embrace your differences, too. Don't shy away from sharing yourself with the world.

10. **Have Grace.** You're name is Lucille Grace for a reason. Be graceful. Be light. Share with the world the love with which you were created.

These few lessons, jotted down over my turkey sandwich, are not everything I wish to impart on you. I'm sure you will hear many, many more opinions from me over the years, but it's a start.

The main thing I want to leave you with is this: you are loved, my little girl. You will make choices that cause you pain. We will cry together. You will hurt me and I will hurt you. We will argue and disagree, probably a lot. If you're anything like me, these fights will be over boys who I think don't deserve you and clothes that are too tight. But we'll also laugh and play. I will always always be here for you no matter what. You are a star! You light up my life. You make me walk on air. I will always see the good in you and you will forever fill up my heart.

Always,
Mom

Mary K. Baxter *Mother, wife, artist, arts administrator, student, teacher, daughter, sister, and friend. Mary, alongside her husband Jesse and her daughter Lucille, works and travels with the international theatre company, Dramatic Adventure Theatre. Here they are on the rim of a volcanic crater lake in the Ecuadorian Andes, their first trip as a family on a lifetime of adventures.*
www.dramaticadventure.com

Story Six

Letter from a Baby Book (1984)

Andrea Hylen

(From Author to her First Born Daughter, Mary)

July 2, 1984
Baltimore, Maryland

Dear Mary,

I have been writing a letter to you in my head since I first became pregnant with you and here you are six months old already. Finally, I am putting my feelings into words and on paper! I want you to know how much I loved being pregnant with you. There were times when I was sick or tired, but I got over those feelings quickly as I thought about you, the baby that was growing inside my belly.

I started to feel you kick in my belly when I was about five months pregnant. I would shout out to your Dad to come into the room and feel you kick. We were like two little kids feeling the joy and excitement. My pregnancy was a happy time for your Dad and me. I want you to know how much we wanted you and still want you in our lives.

Now, here you are six months old and when I think about you I get all choked up with tears because you make me so happy. I want to hug and squeeze you so much all the time. Already, you are becoming an independent lady. You want to do things by yourself, interact with other people and you don't want to be held as much. How can my little baby be growing up so fast?

I hope as you get older that you will keep the disposition that you have now. You are always so happy. Whenever someone needs a smile you come through and flash a love beam at them.

As a parent, all I can do is love you, provide for you and teach you right from wrong. As your parents, I know your Dad and I are going to make a lot of mistakes. Remember we are loving you the best way we know how.

Mary, I hope that you will always talk to us and reach out the way you do now. I hope that you will always be happy, honest, and caring about other people. And remember that you are a gift to us from God. We prayed for you and for your healthiness and God gave you to us.

Love,
Mom

(Andrea Hylen Bio and Photo at the end of the next story)

Story Seven

I Have Nothing Left to Give

Andrea Hylen

January 11, 2014

Thirty years later
Santa Monica, California

"I have nothing left to give."

After 4 months of acquiescing to one of my housemates, I heard those words in my mind on my morning beach walk. What began as one random kindness to welcome my new housemate became a series of silent allowances until I stopped honoring myself. I said, "Yes," to her every request and in the process forgot to take care of my own needs, too. I forgot that taking care of myself is important, too. I forgot how to say, "No." I finally reached a level of frustration and anger one night when I was ready to fall into bed and the things she left in my room blocked the accessibility to my bed and closet. Ahhhhhh!!!! No more people-pleasing, boundary bending, putting her needs in front of mine, sacrificing and building resentment. This had to stop!

As I walked on the beach and heard the words, "I have nothing left to give," it dawned on me like a flash of lightning. Those were the same words playing in my head when I left my first marriage 26 years ago. The interaction with my housemate stirred up similar feelings. Powerlessness. Victimhood. Martydom. Over giving. Mind reading. The gift from my housemate was a wake-up call. I couldn't ignore it for long this time. Wake up and examine that time so many years ago. This was a recurring cycle. This time I had awareness, experience and power. I wanted to look more deeply, find the core wound and learn new skills to explore the feelings.

Leaving my marriage in 1987, brought judgments of "she must be crazy," and fear and withdrawal of support. Yeah, I was crazy to have thought that my husband would stop drinking, stop verbally abusing and criticizing me just because we were married. I was "crazy in love" and blind to the fact that the things that were a challenge before we got married would continue and escalate.

My husband and I were college sweethearts. We had been together for ten years. Both of us had professional jobs. We had two small children and family lineages of marriages that lasted 50+ years. We had numerous examples of couples staying together through thick and thin. Never giving up! The year before we separated I even yelled at a friend on the phone when she told me that she and her husband were going to get a divorce. *"There is no reason for a divorce. You can work through anything!"* How dare she do what I didn't have the courage to do...yet.

A year later, I became the person telling people I was leaving my husband.

The question so many people asked me: "How could you possibly walk out the door and leave your two daughters behind?" I can tell you it was the hardest decision I have ever had to make and all of these years later it is still the hardest thing I ever had to do. There was more pain in that decision than all of the other things that have happened since then; the death of my son, my own life threatening illness, the death of my second husband. It was also the most courageous.

I did it because, "I had nothing left to give." Emotionally, I felt like I crawled out the door, dragged myself to the car, put an oxygen mask to my face and drove my car with metaphorical "flat tires" limping to a house I had rented for my daughters and me.

In my mind, I was the primary caretaking parent and the only one who was "awake" enough to see the destruction of our arguments and fighting in front of our children. Verbal abuse starts out with subtle criticism that attacks a tender heart. My heart was battered and bruised. When I started to voice more of my opinions and talk about ending our marriage, the abuse escalated into physical threats and demonstrations with my husband pinning me into corners and hitting the cabinets behind me. The sound of his fist whizzing by my cheek and even the pop of the beer can sent waves of shock into my body. I knew that I was the target of my husband's frustration and anger.

In order to move things forward and end our marriage, someone had to move out of the house. I didn't see any alternative. And so I did move out, with my husband's full knowledge, on a weekend he took our two daughters to stay with his family. I had every intention of working through the separation details, sharing custody and dissolving our material possessions. I just needed a moment to take a breath and rest.

It didn't go the way I expected. Everything escalated into, "He said, She said." Our family and friends took sides and my husband prepared battle plans. Everyone tried to find out who was wrong and the reasons and they were concerned about my mental health. The communication breakdown that each of us carried into our marriage relationship or people pleasing or denial and all of the other dysfunction, it was all still there. And the other piece was the alcoholism and co-dependency on both sides of the family and my decision to end the marriage stirred up things that everyone tried to deny and stuff down. It stirred up all of the unspoken "elephants" in the room.

Before I walked out, I spent years trying to do everything I could possibly think of to "make my marriage work." I believed being in a marriage meant self-sacrifice and suffering. You made your bed now lie in it. Work through everything. Never give up.

I converted to Catholicism because my husband had been raised Catholic. I felt that if we went to church as a family that would be the solution. I took classes for six months, studying, learning and ready to be a good Catholic. At first it worked. It was a time we all spent together. After the first year, I found myself sitting in church alone in the pew with my two daughters while my husband spent the morning at home alone. He just refused to go to church.

I tried Al-Anon meetings. Two years before I left the marriage, I started attending a lunchtime meeting at the University of Maryland. When I switched jobs to work at Johns Hopkins, I started a lunchtime Al-Anon meeting so I could continue. My husband went to AA a few times and stopped drinking for a short time then decided he wasn't really an alcoholic. He was a hard worker who never missed work. He didn't know the term functional alcoholic.

I went to individual therapy. I studied Family Constellation and learned a lot about people in relationships and the family dynamics I had grown up in. I read the Dance of Anger by Harriet Goldhor Lerner and a variety of other self-help books. Still I was ineffective in "making" my husband communicate with me. Little by little I took on all of the communication responsibility and I tried to do it for us both. I even convinced myself for a period of time that I was an alcoholic because I got drunk at a work party. It felt so good to be irresponsible and let loose. Then, I got scared and attended 90 AA meetings in 90 days. I am not an alcoholic. I am co-dependent. That was the ultimate experience of co-dependency. Trying to work an AA program for someone else!

I don't really know what was going on for my husband. I do know that he worked really hard at his job. Worked long hours and came home, drank beer and went upstairs to his workshop for the rest of the night. I would say that he felt that working and drinking at home made him a good husband and a good father. He took our daughter, Mary to a ballgame when she was a toddler and that was something he enjoyed and probably saw modeled for him. Neither of us had a role model for a mother who worked outside of the home and cared for her children. And he didn't have a model for a woman like me who was social and excited about life who wanted to have neighbors and friends over and who saw life as an adventure. When we got married, I thought we would bundle up our kids in a VW bus and travel. He had adventures like that before we were married, why wouldn't they continue?

I don't know what was going on in his mind because there was no communication until I started to press for conversations and all we did was yell. So, I took action. I left the house. And we spent way too many years fighting over "ownership" of our daughters instead of just loving them. All of these years later, I finally have a term for what happened to me and why I had to leave or die. I am not kidding. That is how extreme it felt and how broken my heart felt. It was the emotional abandonment. His love for me was so palpable and then he took it away.

We separated in 1987, and all of these years later and with all of the healing, it is painful to write this. There was a lot of shame and loneliness. I made a decision that excluded me from day to day contact with my daughters and the pain and loss was excruciating. The legal system in Maryland was clear. The parent who leaves without a separation agreement gets stamped with abandonment. When we finally went to court and the custody situation accelerated, my supervisor at work gave me the best advice of all. He told me to keep being myself. Do the thing I thought was right and let go of the lies that people were saying about me. Let go of the judgments and just keep showing up and being the person I am. He said that some day my daughters would see for themselves. I didn't have to prove anything to anyone. I was there to love and mentor them into adulthood in the best way that I could.

So, I found creative ways to spend time with my daughters on the days they were with my husband. I took a long lunch once a week to go eat with them at the day care center. I rearranged my schedule to work 4 days a week instead of 5 so I could volunteer all day Friday in their elementary schools. I expected that we would celebrate our daughters' birthdays together even after my husband and I both remarried and I made a point of being there no matter what.

I wish I had had the strength and support to work through the child custody and separation before I left the house. I carried the guilt of that for a long time. I don't have any other regrets about leaving.

I remember one morning ten years after the divorce. I was remarried and had given birth to a son and a daughter. My son was born with a congenital heart defect and had died at the age of 19 months. My daughter was healthy and thriving. I had survived a life threatening illness and was now homeschooling our kids. I was lying in bed in the early morning with the sun peaking in through the window and shining on my face. I could feel that I was healed. It was a flash and a knowing sensation in my body. I felt like I had fully returned to myself. I arrived there by reading books, taking personal growth seminars, integrating and practicing and healing and focusing on my own development to be the best role model I could be for my daughters. I wasn't interested in perfection. It was more like authentic, real living and a willingness to change my behavior. I had the desire to be a good role model for my daughters and out of that intention and love for them my life changed. And in the process, I fell in love with myself.

When I read the letter that Mary wrote to her new baby Lucille, my granddaughter, I can tell you that I had the same hopes and dreams. It was in my letter to Mary thirty years ago. (Mary's Letter to Lucille is Story 5. My Letter to Mary is Story 6 in this book)

My hopes and dreams now are that each generation learns from the previous generation and that Mary and her husband Jesse will learn from our mistakes and challenges. I hope that they will listen to the stories, make different choices, feel the love and support that is here for them.

Mary and Jesse are already starting out as parents with more communication skills and more awareness than we had. They will make mistakes and learn something new in the discovery. They are already a co-parenting team and have surrounded themselves with a community of friends and family for support. Much more than my husband and I had in the isolation of our home and marriage.

I can also tell you that my husband became a more involved parent after our divorce. We both fought for our rights to parent and love our children. It's possible that we loved more fiercely. I know I was much more aware of the time I did have with my daughters and the time was more precious. I know that they were loved and held closely.

My husband and I have chosen different paths. Authentically living our lives. We have demonstrated life and choices from two different perspectives. Exposing our children to structure, adventure and love.

Their Dad worked for the government for 30 years and provided a solid home base for our daughters. I have lived the life of an entrepreneur who homeschooled our children for part of their education with innovation and creativity and freedom.

In making the choice to leave, I gave myself the gift to follow my heart, live a life from inspiration and to be courageous in making different choices. I created a new path and demonstrated it for my daughters. They have seen the ups and the downs as I fought to be who I am and to accept and love myself and love them.

In disrupting an old pattern, I have opened another door for them. Now, they get to choose the life they want from the infinite possibilities that are available to them.

Andrea Hylen *believes in the power of a woman's voice to usher in a new world. She is the founder of Heal My Voice, a Minister of Spiritual Peacemaking, a Writing and Transition Coach and Orgasmic Meditation teacher. Andrea has discovered her unique gifts while parenting three daughters and learning to live life fully after the deaths of her brother, son and husband. She is currently living out of a suitcase following her intuition as she collaborates with women and men in organizations and travels around the world speaking, teaching and leading workshops. Her passion is authentically living life and supporting others in doing the same. To connect with Andrea and learn about current projects go to: www.andreahylen.com and www.healmyvoice.org.*

Story Eight

A Potcake is My Heart

Jillian Skalky

My name is Jillian Skalky and I have Crohn's Disease. (Crohn's disease is a form of inflammatory bowel disease (IBD) I was diagnosed at age 12 when I was living in Baltimore. Now I am 22 and I have a service dog named Rosie. I am writing this story to educate people about what it is like to live with a chronic condition and to share my story with people who have similar conditions. I want you to know that good things can always come out of a rough experience. Just because you have a condition, even an invisible one, does not mean you are limited.

Until a year ago I was uncomfortable explaining the definition of Crohn's and how it affected me let alone to explain why I have a service dog. After a decade of having this condition I can finally speak my truth with complete confidence. I can tell people about my experiences in order for them to gain a better understanding of an "invisible disability" and what it really means to live with a chronic condition.

I am one of those Crohn's patients who have experienced every symptom, reaction and side effect; even the rare ones that are not listed. I am the patient who was always calling their doctor on a Friday night in the ER with some erratic emergency. But I have always been the patient that kept fighting and would never let Crohn's take away my life and my spirit. I would never show my pain in school, never express my sickness to family, and even more so, never gave up on my self and what I stand for. But what did I stand for? And who was I fighting for? By April 12, 2013, I finally was forced to let go of my inner fight and let my willingness to surrender lead me to a new path.

When it came to Crohn's, I've been through it all. I was the 7th grader who had golf-ball sized abscesses in the anus. I was the 8th grader who was constipated for a week and had to give myself an enema. I was the 9th grader who would disappear for a month to have my gallbladder removed and tell my classmates that I was just sick. I was the 10th grader who would skip class periodically to get remicade infusions. I was the 11th grader who would sit in the back seat to hide waves of stomach pains as my face turned red as I went into a sweat. I was the 12th grader who couldn't eat wheat, dairy, citrus, tomatoes, and fatty meats. I was the college student who would leave class 10 times to throw up in the closet bathroom. I would skip class because I was in too much pain to get out of bed. I called my doctor every semester for a medical note to waive my attendance for the 30 days of class missed. I was the girl who finally turned on her friends because she was too upset and tired of her own life, even to crack a smile. I was the girl who couldn't hold a job or let people depend on her because of random sick days. I was the girl who had a disability, but never let anyone see her disability.

It wasn't until January 2011 that my fighting spirit gave way and my Crohn's symptoms took over my mind, body, and spirit. All medications failed on me except for Remicade. and after a year of being off the medicine even that didn't work in my favor. On my third infusion I had an anaphylaxis reaction. So no more Remicade.

I was living in Boulder, CO, attending Naropa University. My heart sang in the environment I lived in and I couldn't have been happier. But Crohn's was pulling me away from my ideal life, leading me to a medical withdrawal, and forcing me to fly back to Baltimore in order to treat my condition. I would throw up at the crack of dawn before even drinking water. Gluten free or Dairy free was not cutting it anymore. Anything I ingested, even water, would come right out. Food became my enemy. I would break out in tears at a restaurant because I did not know what I could eat. I became a couch potato. Even a flight of steps would leave me doubled over in pain. Narcotics were my saviors for avoiding ER drama. Sleep was my only friend. The mornings just offered pain and acid pouring out of both ends of my body.

In Baltimore, at age 20, my faithful and most amazing Pediatric GI treated me. After a load of the most disgusting tests, which I had been through countless times, a second surgery became my only option.

On March 11, 2011, I had a section of my terminal ileum and the beginning of my large intestines removed. There were a few setbacks, but in the end I recovered smoothly and by the third week I was eager to return to Boulder.

Within three days of returning, I experienced severe pain and extreme hot flashes and chills. The rush to the ER showed that I had developed a cyst at the site of my last surgery. What I remember from that experience was my friend convincing me to let her take me to the ER, laying in the ER bed being injected with pain killers, then waking up in a room weeks later with an oxygen tube, a PICC line, stitches of course, a J-Pouch, and an Ileostomy.

Apparently many people came to see me, including my mom who flew from Baltimore the moment I called her in the ER. With her by my side, she explained they had to do an exploratory surgery. Crohn's had attacked at the site. I became septic and my body started to deteriorate from the inside. My elevated heart rate, the fluid in my lungs and the pain all came together once they saw the train wreck in my abdominal cavity. Once everything was cleaned up and taken away an ileostomy (temporary) was attached in order for my body to heal.

I don't remember much in the hospital. I don't even remember calling my mom from the ER. A few memories like the hallucinations from the painkillers, being forced to walk in the halls regardless of my excruciating pain, and staring at the Rocky Mountains out of my window. That is all I remember.

Once my mom and I returned to my dorm room everything became real. And real was not a pretty picture. I still remember staring at myself in the mirror with grief and sadness. I was 20 pounds underweight, pale and gaunt with an oxygen tube and picc line for a month, and now a bag covering the pink, wet stoma sticking out of my stomach. I was disgusted with myself. And for a moment, I wished I had never survived the surgery. Life became even more of a struggle with a bag leaking, stitches re-opening, limping from room to room, being bathed by my mother and a nurse injecting antibiotics every morning and night. I hid from my friends, ashamed of my current state. It took a good month to even leave my dorm and face the world. Covering my PICC line with a sleeve I knitted, I walked through the farmers market, drove up the mountains to taste the fresh air and even started a knitting project; a fisherman's sweater that occupied most of my healing time when I wasn't sleeping.

Months later I chose to take a year off from school to heal. I moved to Florida to spend time with my brothers and dad and soak up the healing sun. Even after a year of rest, I did not truly start to heal until March 10, 2012 when I adopted a puppy: my Potcake Rosie.

Now for the real story!

Rosie is a rescue from the Bahamas. The name Potcake is given to these street dogs because the islanders feed them cake-like leftover rice from the bottom of a pot. Rosie, like many Potcakes, didn't start out with a happy beginning. The dogs are abandoned and left to scavenge for food in the blistering sun left only to live a few years until infection or heat gets the best of them. Or worse, the authorities shoot them for being a nuisance.

Rosie, along with her siblings, was found only a few weeks old in a landfill. They were shipped to south Florida where our paths crossed.

I am a Golden Retriever dog at heart but refused to buy a dog. The first time I saw Rosie's little gangly body and huge puppy eyes I fell in love. From the moment I took her home, we were never apart. It is as if we share the same soul and separating us is a pain we could not bare. The possibility of Rosie becoming my service dog didn't blossom until she was around six months old because who ever heard of a service dog for a Crohn's Patient?

October 2012 was my wake-up call. I developed an abscess near my ostomy and it quickly needed to be removed. Since my surgery in Boulder, my fighting spirit had switched to fear and panic. I did not embrace the daily challenges Crohn's offered but hid under the blanket. When I was recovering from that little surgery I began searching for service dog trainers. Luckily enough I found someone an hour north who would train a dog for a person who has any disability, Crohn's, Autism, Diabetes, Epilepsy. All I needed was a doctor's note. From that moment on, the trainer, Rosie and I worked together to create the service dog she is today. Now mind you it was not an easy task, but it was all worth it.

Now Rosie truly goes everywhere with me; from grocery store, to the Hospital, to my Grandparent's Club House.

So let me ask, what defines a service dog?

I was not able to fully answer this question myself until a few days ago while celebrating Passover with my family.

I love my family and I know that I have not explained my Crohn's experience to them, and not shared the gruesome details of my condition. I chose this purely because I refused to be looked at as a disabled person and being pitied.

So to them, all of a sudden I had a service dog. It is common to see someone who is blind or in a wheel chair with a Service Dog, but not someone who has Crohn's or a Gastrointestinal illness.

So all of a sudden my disability became visible because I never truly shared my experience with them and how Crohn's took away so much of my life and capabilities. I should not have expected them to understand. In the past I would not have invited them to ask questions, but now...bring it on!

The first reaction from some of my family:
I don't need a service dog because I am not blind or in a wheel chair.

Then an annoyance: *"Do you have to bring the dog everywhere?"*

At first, I reacted with a lot of emotion. I realized they don't know who I really am based on the experiences I endured. How could they know when I refused to share?

I have had to become used to strangers sneering at me for bringing a dog in the restaurant or being taken aback by me requesting that they do not pet my dog. If someone has been conditioned a certain way, like we all have, it's hard to shift to a different way of being or understanding. But all we have to do is be open, and then we can learn so much more!

During my families' visit in Florida, I explained my condition step by step; what I experience, and how Rosie helps me.

Here are some of the reasons I need a service dog:

1. Getting help: Rosie can identify people by name. Most importantly my mom, Liz. If I am stuck somewhere, and can't shout for help because of the pain I will tell Rosie to "get help and find Liz." She will find my mom

and bark for her attention, bringing my mom to me. In a public place, I can even write a "help" note, put it in her mouth and search for someone to give it to.

2. During post operative, or painful moments, I can ask her to retrieve important items, like my phone, medicine, ostomy bag, or anything that is light enough for her to pick up. I do have some lazy moments and ask her to fetch me the TV remote.

3. Sometimes I can't bend down or move my body without experiencing pain. Rosie will then pick anything up for me and bring it to my level so I don't have to move. She will even help undress me. Reaching to take off socks can be a painful task.

4. Another helpful tool that I taught her was scent training. Many people with Epilepsy or Diabetes have scent-trained dogs to alert them before they have a seizure or have a high/low in blood sugar levels. Because a Crohn's Flare-Up is not necessarily a "chemical reaction" it was difficult to train her to alert my symptoms. What I did train her to do was to alert me before my ostomy bag leaked. It was a complete shot in the dark but so far she has alerted me to over a dozen times my bag has leaked. Normally medical alert dogs will bark or put their paws on the owner to alert them of the change. Rosie has her own method and jumps up to me, puts her nose right to my bag, and licks her chops. Then I know within ten minutes my bag will leak.

5. Her simple presence and unconditional love has pushed me past many dark moments and frustrating times during the constant struggle of having Crohn's. Having my Rose snuggle with me in the hospital bed makes the stress of getting sick all that more manageable.

Today, I am continuing to move my life forward. After two years of being out of school, I plan to enroll at a Florida International University doing what I love, Visual Arts and teaching Children with Disabilities.

While Rosie continues to take care of me, I do my best to take care of others with her as my guide. I take Rosie through the hospital and see faces light up. I attend events like Surfer for Autism or the Gumbo Limbo Nature Center. Her presence lights up the faces of so many people who like me have been through hard times and just need a bit of unconditional love sent their way.

A service dog can do so much for someone with any shape of a disability. You could be blind or in a wheelchair. You could have anxiety or a learning disability or even a GI illness. As long as that dog aids you in the help you need it is serving you. Respecting a service dog and the work they do for their owner is respecting that person with a disability, no matter what disability they carry. But keep in mind that even though a service dog may make that person's disability visible, it does not define who they are. An illness or condition is only like the clothes on their back, a part of them, but not who they are.

Keep a watchful eye out for those who fake having a service dog by putting a vest on their pet. I know just about all dog owners would love to take their dogs everywhere with them, but what they are doing is pretending to have a disability. They are putting their dogs and the public at risk by having a dog not trained to behave appropriately in public. By turning a blind eye to their actions, owners who invest in having a trained service dog are more easily discriminated against and are harassed in public which doesn't allow their service dog to do the job they were trained for. True service dogs, even once certified are constantly being trained so that they can always be prepared to handle the unpredictability that public places can bring.

For me, I would never wish away having Crohn's. Although it has put me through hard times and torturing experiences without it I would not be the person I am today. Each experience has taught me something new and led me to a more authentic path. Having Rosie as my service dog has opened my eyes and encouraged me to follow my heart. I am right where I'm supposed to be. And so are you.

Jumping a year forward...

Rosie and I are still partners in crime, always together and supporting each other. A couple months ago I had another surgery where they removed more infected intestines and gave me a new stoma. Rosie was by my side the whole time helping me recover slowly back to health. I am also happy to say that for the first time in my life I am both in school full time and working full time. I am on my way to achieving my Bachelors of Fine Arts (BFA). True, it's not at a hot-shot art institute like I would have chosen 4 years ago, but all that matters to me is that I am practicing my art because its what I love.

Now my new job and new passion is helping others with disabilities by training service dogs. My boss, Jason, who helped me train Rosie, must have been impressed by how fast I trained her and offered me a position with his company. It's the perfect job for me where I create my own schedule, Therefore having Crohn's will not affect my work. I work with children and adults to help create the relationship between service dog and owner like I have with Rosie. And the best part is I work with dogs all day, so I am constantly surrounded with unconditional love and wet kisses.

Before my emergency surgery in 2011, I did not expect my life to be on this path. Having Crohn's forced me to open my horizons and allow life to happen.

I am living in my joy and couldn't be happier.

Jillian Skalky is 23 years old who has struggled with Crohn's Disease since the age of 12. Despite her condition she has followed her own path doing what she loves: working with animals and creating art. She studied since the age of 15 in the visual arts, focusing in the medium of sculpture, painting and traditional photography. She currently attends college, and despite Crohn's causing set backs in her graduation, she still pushes forward to gain her Bachelors in Fine Arts. Her new passion and career involves training dogs to be service dogs. Even though working with dogs all day and being a full-time art student Jillian enjoys spending her free time out in nature, gardening or raising live-stock, to be more sustainable on Mother Earth.

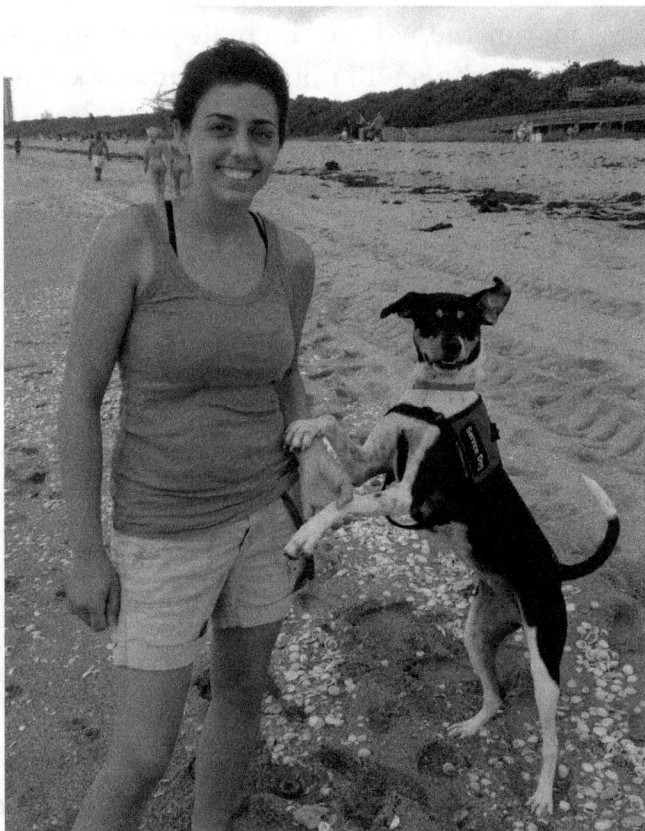

Story Nine

The Mother's Eyes

Liz Draman

From the moment our eyes met I felt the sacred bond between a mother and child that transcends the human experience - ignite in my heart. It was love at first sight!

The most powerful karmic relationships that we can experience are those between parents and their children. Mother-daughter relationships are complex and diverse. Some mothers and daughters are best friends. Others talk once a week. Some see each other often; others live thousands of miles away. Some bicker regularly while others avoid conflict. And then there are those who, like my daughter and I, are deeply aware of our soul agreement and consciously live in honor of it. Indeed, the bond between a mother and daughter runs deeper than a physical connection.

Souls who incarnate as women have chosen a special role in the evolution of humankind. We are the face of the Divine Feminine at a time when the world we live in demands balance of the Masculine and Feminine energies. We see this play out as the archaic Patriarchal Archetypes of the world are crumbling and in its dust emerges the Age of ReUnion. I believe the reunion occurring is within each of us. Women are the catalyst for this shift as we are the ones carrying the seeds of the Divine Feminine in the womb of our creations. We are here to awaken the archetype of The Mother in us, and as we do The Mother wakes up in our world. One can feel her rolling over at times gently stirring us to change, other times fiercely stripping the veils of illusion from our human skin. Yet, in every experience Her Love Calls us to open our heart and embody the Divine Qualities of our Mother's Essence – Mercy, Power, Strength, Reciprocity, Authority, Purity, Beauty, Tenderness, and for me, in this story, Compassion like I have never known.

For most of my adult life I have walked very comfortably in my masculine energy. It wasn't until the age of 49 that I was ready to begin seeing my world through The Mother's Eyes. What follows is an account of one of many rites of passage in the sacred journey of a mother and daughter - daughter and mother's compassionate awakening.

I dedicate my story to The Mother in you:

April 2011

Sitting at the breakfast table in my daughter's dorm room at

Naropa University in Boulder, Colorado the aroma of coffee brewing and the early morning sunlight shining through the window quietly wakes my weary body. My majestic new friends, the Rocky Mountains await my arrival for our morning communion. Since landing here two weeks ago they have been my source of strength as I walk uncharted territory with my sweet child.

One month earlier…

My phone rings. On the other end, I hear my daughter's trembling voice barely audible whispering "Mom, I'm headed to the ER at Boulder Community Hospital. Please come".

This is the call all parents hope never to get. Since she was diagnosed with Crohns dis-ease at age 12, we're veterans to ER visits and hospital stays. This call was different. My little girl was 2500 miles away. Just three weeks before, on March 11, 2011, Jill had a colon resection surgery in Baltimore, MD and, in her tenacious style, was eager to jump fully into life after just three weeks of recovery. Nothing holds her down. My older sister who mothered me as a wild teenager year old would lecture "adversity builds character." Now, my daughter for such contrasting reasons teaches me how "graceful character gets you through adversity".

Arriving at the Denver airport the next day I was met by one of Jillian's guardian angels. Amanda a childhood friend, who always seems to be with Jill at just the right moment, was now there for me. Mothering is an innate instinct that is not limited to age, relationship or gender; it's a primal instinct stirred when someone we love is in need. One day during the summer of 2009, Amanda kept Jill company for one of her seven hour Remicade infusions, which unexpectedly caused an anaphylactic reaction; which is a serious, potentially life-threatening allergic response. Amanda in her calm demeanor called the nurse and casually saved my daughter's life. Two years later she just happened to transfer to Naropa University and popped in to see Jill finding her in her dorm room quite ill. Like a mother-hen, she insisted on taking Jill to the ER.

Children who deal with chronic pain develop a high tolerance and sometimes underestimate the severity of their symptoms. Pain becomes just another part of life. At times I felt anger for the constant presence of pain in my daughter's life. I believe what I experienced in this story opened a crack in my consciousness that made it possible for me to uncover deeply buried feelings of anger and dare I say *hate* for the pain women have endured throughout the centuries. We must be willing to journey into the darkest chambers of our heart to unleash the magnitude of love we have inside us.

Not knowing what to expect, I anxiously stepped into the lobby of Boulder Community Hospital and was struck by the beautiful vista through the floor to ceiling windows. The Rocky Mountains stood as sentinels in the distance. My heart leapt and tears rolled down my face. I'm not sure if my reaction was from sheer exhaustion or the deep sense that I was truly in a healing place.

When I walked into Jill's room she was heavily sedated and hooked up to IV's and a variety of monitors I had not seen before. Slowly opening her big chocolate chip eyes, she smiled and whispered, "Mommy, you came!" "Of course I came silly, I love you" I replied. I heard in her voice a deeper meaning to her surprised greeting. It would take over two years for the significance of her words to be revealed.

Her team of doctors paraded into the room and began updating me on her status. As they explained the severity of her state I felt my body give way to the chair behind me. I

could not believe what I was hearing. After an initial CAT scan, a dime size cyst was found located at the incision of her colon reconnection causing an inferno of infection. How can something so small have wreaked so much havoc in her body? Seeing her Mom walk into the room was the last recollection she had of the next ten days. Like a protective mother, her mind shielded the memory of this experience from her consciousness. I would be her witness, her advocate, her strength, her voice of love. My place in her soul's journey became swiftly apparent. My identity as mother, giver of life, fell away. The power of her infinite soul filled the room as
I stood by her bed and realized how little control I had over her life. While my sweet girl fought the fire of infection ravaging her body, my greatest service to her was to be strong and pray.

Each day I took solace walking the labyrinth in the beautiful hospital courtyard. I poured my heart out to the spirit of the mountains and emptied myself at the feet of Sacred Earth Mother. I believe she heard me and I felt she would soon answer. It is said that above every hospital there abides one or more Angel Devas of Healing and uncountable Legions of Healing Angels providing assistance to our medical world. I felt their presence and let in the healing I was there to receive, too.

One afternoon returning from a particularly powerful heart chakra opening while sitting in the middle of the labyrinth, a nurse stopped me in the hall and asked me to have a seat. Jill had become septic. They were prepping Jill for surgery. It was clear to me the connectedness I felt to Divine Mother that day was preparation for what was to come.

No matter how many times a mother waits for her child to come out of surgery it feels like the first time. Five hours later, the surgeon found me in Jill's room and gave her report.

Although she explained the potential scenarios, when the least desirable option is necessary, it still comes as a shock. I was not ready to hear the surgeon say she had to perform an ileostomy on my daughter's beautiful body. Now more than ever it was time to call up my strength.

Three days after the surgery, an ostomy nurse came in to support Jill with learning how to care for her stoma and change her j-pouch. This was the first time we saw her stoma since the surgery. I'm not a squeamish girl, but seeing my precious child's intestines pulled from her belly was more than I could handle. I felt like I would to pass out and wanted to run out of the hospital room but remained calm until the nurse left. Jill quickly fell asleep which was my opportunity to run. I got in my car and drove. I had no idea where I was going but I found a spot to park on a quiet street in downtown Boulder and just sobbed. This was all just too much. I was alone; sleep deprived and felt deep grief. I gave it all to the spirit of the mountains.

The first week home Jill and I laid in her dorm bed together, it was now her moment to sob. I held her in my arms while she wept. Physically exhausted, I had nothing left to give. In a time when she needed me the most all I could do was hold her. Like a child myself, I called silently to The Mother. "I can't do this, help me." In that moment I felt an immediate answer to my Call.

My body ignited with heat. My eyes got blurry. I felt disoriented so I shut them tight to refocus and when I opened them, I looked down at my hands; they were not my own. I looked at Jill and realized I was not seeing her through my eyes. I was not touching her with my hands. I was truly filled with a Presence I innately recognized as Divine Mother energy.

And as this energy of love filled my heart with peace

and strength, I truly saw my daughter as a child of God.

From that moment I was not the same. A hidden chamber of my soul was touched, liberating the tender heart I had worked so hard to hide. This was the beginning of the awakening of my Divine Mother Love.

Six weeks later...

Sitting at the breakfast table in my daughter's dorm room preparing to return to my life, the aroma of coffee brewing and the early morning sunlight shining through the window warms my soul. I turn and bow in gratitude to the ever present spirit of the Mountains which are alive with the heartbeat of the sacred Mother.

Through The Mother's Eyes I now see, I AM the sacred bond between The Mother and Child that transcends the human experience.

***Liz Draman** was inspired to create her vision, Awaken to Love as a movement toward living from the heart of who you are ~ illuminating a path to your inner brilliance and conscious living. She is a passionate awakener of Conscious Love, Light and Life and an active teacher committed to spiritual education and empowering women to awaken their Divine-Power. www.lizdraman.com*

Liz is dedicated to walking this scared path in own life and for the past 24 years has shared the journey with the joy of her life, her daughter Jillian.

Part Three

I AM Generous

"In the end, though, maybe we must all give up trying to pay back the people in this world who sustain our lives. In the end, maybe it's wiser to surrender before the miraculous scope of human generosity and to just keep saying thank you, forever and sincerely, for as long as we have voices."

— Elizabeth Gilbert

Story Ten

I Am Finally Home!

Nukhet Govdeli Hendricks

It was Friday, October 8, 2010. I had just left a meeting and saw there were 6 missed calls on my cellphone, all from my sister who was living in Turkey and a voice message. The voice message was from my niece asking me to call them. I heard the urgency in her tone of voice. My heart knew I was about to get the news that was going to break my heart into pieces and that my life was never going to be the same again.

When I called back and heard my sister's voice, what I knew in my heart was affirmed. My mother was gone. She had passed away three hours ago. Mom did not suffer my sister said; it happened really fast, she was gone in minutes. I couldn't hear the rest because all I could hear was the sound of my heart beating. I wondered how my heart could still beat with such determination.

What followed this heart piercing news was the *final part of a life-long journey* to re-connect to my essence, to learn the meaning of self-love, self-compassion and tender self-embrace. This is the story of this journey.

I was born in Adana, Turkey. As a child, I was an empath, extremely intuitive, sensitive to the energies around me and I talked to the angels to boot. I could carry on long and delightful conversations with the angels. The adults thought I was talking to my imaginary friends. However, none of this was in my conscious awareness. It was who I was, natural as breathing, and there was no reason to question it. But this also made it rather difficult to manage everyday life, for I was extremely sensitive to other people's energies around me, to the fluctuations in weather and the humidity. I had to create a system to manage all this as well as to survive in the noisy outside world. As long as I knew I could come home and hide behind my books and studies, have alone and quiet time, I could survive a few noisy and chaotic hours out there in school. The end result of this system was that I was an extremely successful student.

Summer months were my favorite. My mother, an elementary school teacher, would have the entire summer off and bring home dozens of books from the school library for us to read during the long hot summer days. I absolutely loved our "siesta" time from 12pm to 3-4 pm in the afternoon. That meant my mom got to have all the time she needed for herself. My sister and I were to be quiet, take a nap, read a book, but spend time alone. My favorite activity during out "siesta" time was reading. I could read an entire book in one day, and still be starving for more books to read. Those days were the most delicious days of my childhood.

I was in awe of my mother. She was a mystery to me. She could draw like a dream. She was also an incredible tailor, with a skill almost second to none, and her fashion drawings were breathtaking. One minute I would watch her draw this incredibly beautiful summer dress, and within days my sister or I or my Mother would be wearing it. She had a great sense of humor, laughed easily and freely.

Then I turned 14 and everything abruptly changed. Suddenly there was no quiet time, no fashion drawings coming alive in pretty colored slippery silks and soft as a dream muslins; no more endless supply of books to lose ourselves in. My mother was suddenly too busy with "things" … and I was expected to follow suit. I thought it was odd that I couldn't continue the valuable practice of retreating to my room for quiet time, because I was being asked to do more: more housework, more help in the kitchen, on and on. It seemed we were repeating the same things over and over again every day but we could never catch up with the housework, the cleaning, the ironing, the cooking. There was no time for anything else, let alone time for me, for her, for reading, for laugher or for fun. Most upsetting of all, I was asked to stop talking to my imaginary friends, because 14 year old girls did not have imaginary friends. So that was also the beginning of shutting out the life-giving and affirming voices of the angels.

It was rather curious that being a girl-child came with the privilege of me time and freedom to talk to the angels, but the cost of growing up as a girl was giving up all these privileges that sustained my soul and who I am. I somehow learned that I must wait for permission to be given so that I can have my quiet siesta times back. Of course the permission never came. I watched my mother slowly lose her health, her joy, her laughter, as she was busy, spending all her time working, doing household chores with the meticulousness of a surgeon, cooking, washing clothes, waiting on my father hand on foot. I remember her even laying clean clothes on the bed for my father so that he can easily find them after his shower. I was looking at my future unfold through my mother. I remember asking my mother about this many years later. I asked her if she had any songs left unsung. She told me all about the responsibilities she had, leaving no time for "herself" and for the things she so wanted to do. Yes, she did have her songs in her still: she so wanted to travel more, spend more time on the beach, visit her brothers in Germany and in other parts of Turkey, and open up her own tailor shop. But there was no time to sing her songs, because she had to take care of Dad, my sister and me. That did not leave her anytime for anything else. At the time, not knowing any better, I decided right there and then that I will never have children! Having children meant complete loss of freedom, loss of the self. Having my sister and me had cost my mother her songs. I never had biological children*

So, my mother's normal became my normal too. I was too young to demand time to get to know the 14-year girl who was evolving to be a young woman. The only way to survive this was to "shut" down the empath part of me because the empath part of me was miserable without quiet time to rejuvenate and to dream! It was either be miserable all the time or go numb. Numb I went. It took work, but I did it. I didn't know it then of course, but this was simply killing my spirit with my own hands.

I got older, left home to go to college 400 miles away despite my mother's objections to my being so far away from home. In my mind, the only way to find myself and get to know me was to put some miles between my mother and myself. But the sad part was that I had already checked out of my own life. I just didn't know it.

For a long time, I really didn't know what happened when I turned 14 that everything changed so drastically. For years, I thought it was my Mother giving into the pressures of Society and giving up her individuality. She gave up her "self" and her freedom in the name of conforming and making sure we conformed to the norm with her. She made sure we did not have any unrealistic expectations: we certainly could not assume that our "adulthood" would have room for the "self."

No denying there was some truth to that, but I did not realize the true reason behind it all until one day I found myself in the United States, married for four years, in small-town America. I realized I was living my mother's life with my alcoholic husband, minus the two kids my mother had. Then I understood. The year I turned 14, my mother gave in; she accepted her fate that she was in a marriage where she had no control over my dad's alcoholism. Alcoholism was not even -acknowledged- back then, let alone treated. My mother simply gave in. You see, it is so much easier to be in –motion-; in "do" mode when you have surrendered to a life spiraling out of your control, so you don't have to stop and think that you are living a life you no longer enjoy or sustains you.

Divorce was not an option for my mother. Not that she was not financially independent, mind you. Her teacher's income would have taken care of her and us. It was simply not an option in the 1970's Turkey. Good women did not divorce their husbands. So, since she couldn't control my dad's drinking, she needed to control everything else around her, and that included my sister and me. Which meant we shut down everything that makes us "us", got into the "do" mode, and sacrificed the "self" for the sake of survival.

This realization came when I found myself trying to control everything else around me because I was unable to control my ex-husband's drinking. It took me another six years to have the courage to realize that the marriage was over. Here I was: 38 years old, thousands of miles away from my birth country, living in a small town in the US, with three cats and a dog. I finally had the courage to free myself from the marriage ties that bound me and I was lost - completely lost. This was in 1998.

I remember my mother's anger when she heard that I was getting a divorce. I knew it would be hard for her. I was doing something she wished she had, but never did.

You see, my relationship with my mother had become very strained after I moved out of the house to go to college, and then to the USA, never to return home to live. The more my mother wanted to pull me back home, the more I pulled away. She used every opportunity to tell me that this was proof I did not care about my family. She was always sad or worried. She held on to that –worry- and –sadness- like it was a lifeline. She simply no longer knew how to live without worrying and being sad about one thing or another. She firmly believed the biggest reason for her life being sad and incomplete was that I was not living in our hometown. And with my divorce, I had delivered one big blow. It came to the point that even when there was a glimmer of joy and happiness, she made sure that these feelings were simply fleeting. She wore the sadness and unhappiness like a cloak that protected-her from what, I'm not sure.

Fast forward to 2007, I was married to the love of my life for five years, still living in small-town USA. I was happy, or so I was thinking, but I was feeling like I am not 100% there: not in my marriage, not in my work, not in my own life. My life was feeling two sizes too small. I had a vague idea that a vital part of me was missing. It was as if I was living my life outside, looking-in. So I found myself searching for "it." At the same time I was beginning to notice the intuitives and angel communicators in my community. Something about them felt very familiar but I couldn't put my finger on it.

One night, I went to bed feeling rather unsettled. In my dream, I heard a voice, gentle and quiet at first saying "listen to your heart". I did not pay attention the first time I heard it, nor the second time. But the third time, the voice was so loud when "it" said "listen to your heart" that I became fully awake and shot up in bed. There was no one in the room other than my husband sleeping peacefully, but I knew we were not alone. I smell the roses and I realized I already knew the voice. It was the voice I had shut down when I turned 14. I whispered, "I heard you"; the voice whispered back "Good, now go back to sleep"... I could hear the sigh of relief and the smile in the voice. I had finally heard the angels again, 32 years after I shut them down and went numb when I was 14.

I spent the next three years, thinking I was embracing my entire being, listening to my heart but I still was not responding to the divine messages I kept getting and I was thinking that I can re-learn "self-love and acceptance" without embracing my gift of communicating with the angels... still caught between that push and pull... love the self, deny the self. I was making some progress, but still uncomfortable about completely letting go, afraid to soften up and become vulnerable ... afraid to embrace 100% of who I was... I didn't even dare.

Then on Feb 16, 2009, my father passed away. My dad's spirit came for a visit to say goodbye before he transitioned. It was unlike anything I had ever experienced. I felt utter and complete connection with my father's spirit through the divine. Moments after this encounter with my father's spirit, my sister's phone call confirmed that our father had indeed passed away. It rocked me to my core. And I realized that there was no turning back. I could no longer deny the fact that I was a direct channel and pure vessel to the divine. But I still did not know what to do about it. I couldn't breathe.

In the meantime, my mother who was having health issues for years was getting worse. She had lost her independence due to her health issues. She could no longer live alone and had moved in with my sister and her family. She was miserable every day, and in constant complaint mode. She was living in the past and recounting every single wrong doing that she was dealt by life and others. There was no consoling her. I went to visit her in May 2010 for Mother's Day. It broke my heart to see her so miserable. In the meantime, my sister who followed our mother's and my footsteps and married an alcoholic as well was having her own issues with her own husband. I felt it in my bones as I visited the four of them; my mother, my sister, my niece, and my brother-in-law; there was no peace, no serenity. Four strangers in one place thrown together by karma. The woman I first met in my childhood; my mother; was completely lost. There was not even a spark of who she was in her eyes. It was now filled with excruciating grief of a life lived on auto pilot. She simply couldn't comprehend doing anything that brought her joy. Her reason for living was to be in a constant state of grief: grief of a husband who was now gone, grief of a life unlived.

My heart broke as I left. In the corner of my heart, there was this fear that this might be the last time I saw her. Sure enough, exactly five months to the day after I left my mother in Turkey, I got the phone call. She was gone.

I flew home in a hurry for the funeral; went on auto-pilot to support my sister and everyone else, checking out of my body to simply survive. I wondered as I sat through all the funeral-related activities; did my mother have a single moment of happiness in her life? Was she ever happy?

As I was flying back home to the US, my heart was filled with an incredible heaviness. This was beyond grief. I felt an immense sadness for my mother's life that was lived in a perpetual state of grief. It broke my heart to think of my mother as a little girl, filled with dreams of a happy life, never even imagining that it would turn out this way. And then I was filled with incredible anger about the fact that she did not take control of her life. Instead of trying to control everyone around her, she could have taken control of her life, design a life that made her happy. She could have given herself permission to LOVE herself as much as she claimed to love us.

I spent another four months or so with my heart breaking into thousands of pieces for her every day. I was torn between sadness, compassion and anger for her. I was angry because she simply stopped living her life; stopped tending to her own spirit and waited for someone to give her permission to "live" joyfully. I was sad because my mother, a woman with incredible gifts and talents and so much to offer to the world died long before her physical body left on October 8, 2010. I felt compassion for her because, somehow she simply didn't know how to climb out of the dark hole she fell into when I turned 14. My heart ached for her. Every night in my dreams, I reached out for the little girl my mother was and rocked her.

Then one day, I heard myself telling a friend to stop waiting for permission to live her life. The moment that came out of my mouth, I felt frozen with the realization that I have been doing exactly the same thing … waiting for permission to let go of the guilt, the sadness and the anger I felt for my mother because she did not choose to love herself enough to sing her songs. I was not allowing myself joy and happiness. I was hiding behind the sadness and the anger instead of reaching deep within to reconnect to my spirit. I was avoiding living fully. I was waiting for permission to live my life. This hit me hard. It brought me down to my knees. Finally, after 35 years; I realized that I can no longer pretend I was living a life of my own choosing. I was living my mother's life. Year 2011.

Since then, I have been on an incredibly scary journey! I am slowly getting to know the real me! I am no longer asking for permission to be who I am. I am simply being who I am. No apologies, no excuses, no explanations. I am slowly letting go of the need that it is my responsibility and duty to keep everyone happy. I am turning the responsibility of their own happiness to them, and claiming the responsibility of my own happiness. I am saying 'no' when I want to say 'no' and I mean it. Now my "yes"s are more meaningful. I am realizing that I like the woman I am becoming. I am beginning to soften around the edges. Like Lauren Bacall said; I am no longer a has been, I AM a "becoming" and a will be. I am a beautifully unfinished woman, tasting the deliciousness and the juiciness of living a life on my own terms. I am no longer sad for my mother or for her unsung songs or sad life. I am learning that I am capable of loving myself enough both for my mother and myself. I can honor my mother's unlived life, unsung songs, by living my life deliciously and singing my own songs. I am feeling the deep love and compassion for my mother I thought I've lost during the long hot summer of my 14th year old youth. I AM becoming my mother's SONG! I AM becoming my own beautiful SONG! Above all, I AM remembering who I was before I was told who I should be!

Here I am - 52 years old - finally seeing "ME" when I look at the mirror. I know the woman who is looking back at me intimately. I smile at the image on the mirror, and she smiles back with eyes shining bright, alive with love and living! The voice whispers; "we've just begun, best is yet to come".

*When I married my husband in 2002, he gave me the gift of his beautiful daughter Abby. As I write my story, she is 18 years old, growing in to a beautiful young lady, living with us and getting ready for college.

Nukhet Govdeli Hendricks, is a gifted intuitive who channels the divine guidance of the angels and the dolphins for those who are seeking to gain clarity to live their most spirited and sparkling lives. It is Nukhet's soul mission to be a bridge to the angelic realm; to assist others on their path to divine love and light, and to connect them to their innermost wisdom, that divine spot within. Nukhet, a native of Turkey who moved to the USA in 1987, lives in West Fargo, ND with the love of her life husband Bryan, daughter Abby, and her cats Hobo and Kiki. Visit Nukhet's website at www.nukhets.com.

Story Eleven

Generations: The Evolution of Love

Karen A. Porter

"Hi, I'm Karen."

A first interaction is usually an introduction. I tell you my label. When the boys were young, I was sometimes "Anton's Mom" or "Sasha's Mom" and lately, in hospitals and in funeral homes, I have been someone's daughter, sister, sister-in-law, or niece. My first role was being Norbert and Oriole's daughter. A friend once distinguished me as her friend with the oddest named parents.

My father, Norbert John Porter, was born June 6, 1924 and as was a practice in Polish Catholic families, he was named for the Saint whose feast day it was. This started a lineage of Norberts in the family.

When your name is Norbert, you can be Norbert or Norb. My brother was Norby to some and the moniker 'Little Norb' has been used as more Norberts entered the family (there are four generations of Norberts so far). So formally, my father was known as Mr. Porter, Mr. Norbert, or Mr. Norb. His mother and wife both called him Norbert. My sister's husband Ted called him "the father" and my sons called him 'Doshka' short for "Dyadoshka," Russian for grandfather. Most of the family called him "Pop". To my husband David, he was "Dad" and to my sister Emily and me, he was "Daddy." Regardless of what he was called, Norbert Porter was known to everyone as a hard working man defined by his sense of duty, honor and strong will.

When Daddy was a very young boy, his older brother James had rheumatic fever. For years after, Grandmom had Daddy physically carry Uncle James to 'save his heart.' While favoritism for the oldest son surfaced regularly, this task laid the foundation for my father's world view. He became physically strong beyond his years, he took on the responsibility for saving his older brother as a duty. He did not question and he did not complain.

Dad's family lived off the land. His parents met while their families worked area farms. When the Porters saved enough money, they bought land on a peninsula in an inlet of the Chesapeake Bay. They started a bathing beach, fished, hunted and guided fishing and hunting parties. Dad made Christmas wreaths each year, from scratch, first finding the boughs to bend into circle forms, then gathering crows-foot, bundling the sprigs into bunches and tying the bunches onto the forms. Time consuming, labor intensive and beautiful when done, Dad and his brothers made multiple grosses to sell wholesale to Baltimore City market vendors. For years, they sold the wreaths for twenty five cents a dozen. When they were offered a dollar a dozen, they dove into wreath making with renewed fervor. Big money! Unquestioning hard work.

Mommy and Daddy met in school, were sweethearts and graduated in the fateful class of 1942. Dad joined the navy and served as a gunner in the Pacific. He did not talk about the war very much at all but he did tell of being strapped to his gun and fighting through the night, witnessing Kamikaze pilots and being in Japan after Hiroshima and Nagasaki. Strength, duty, honor, will.

After the war, Norbert and Oriole were married and had Emily and then Norb. With his brothers, Dad started a construction firm. As the business grew, my parents built their brick home next to another brick house built by and for a younger brother. Our family grew with my birth and then Dan's. When my uncle relocated his family, Grandmom moved in next door and Dad assumed the role of caregiver.

I was young when Norb and his wife Linda learned why their almost three year old daughter wasn't walking. The diagnosis was hydrocephalus. She needed serious surgery and even then, she might never walk. Dad calmly declared, "Then we'll carry her for the rest of her life." Strength, duty, honor, will.

One day, years later, Dad came home in the middle of the day. He saw smoke coming from Grandmom's house. She had fallen asleep with a pot on the stove. He pulled her out of the house, saving her life and went back in to put out the fire. The family repaired the house and after months in a burn unit, Grandmom lived at home for three more years before she passed. Dad had been hospitalized with some burns and lung damage that contributed to his developing COPD. No regrets, no complaints. You do what you have to do.

Mommy loved us; she was the heart of the family. She cried the tears, orchestrated family get-togethers and passed on traditions. Daddy championed us. He was the will. He was behind us and beside us doing whatever he could do to support each of us in what we needed to do and what we wanted to do. We went into the world with jobs, businesses; we married, built homes, and had families.

When David and I told the family about our plans to adopt and that we were in the pilot program for adoption from the Soviet Union, everyone was worried. Except Daddy. He told me not to worry about anything. He was sure that any child who had lived through early trauma and survived institutionalization would be fine. "The Russians are sturdy stock," he said.

In addition to strength, honor and will, Dad had faith. Strong faith. Unwavering faith. Faith in God, faith in himself and faith in us that we could do what we needed to do and that everything would be fine. We buried Dad holding his prayer book. It was well worn and tattered, far from physical beauty yet surpassingly exquisite as it showed his faith and devotion in tangible form.

From early 2000 to April 2002, Daddy cared for Mommy during her battle with breast cancer. He prayed for the "Dear Lord" to take him along with Mom. Even before Mom passed, Dad prayed to die. It took eleven years for that prayer to be answered. During those years, we fulfilled our promises to Mom that we would take care of Daddy.

Taking care of Dad was a duty. I had made a promise. It became a burden. I got very sick and learned I had to take care of myself. Dad was miserable, sad and lonely. They had made a home in an isolated area. While Mom was social and kept them connected to friends and life, once Mom passed, Dad was lost and unwilling to change.

The first three anniversaries of Mom's death, Dad spent in the hospital. The first year, Dad had bleeding ulcers. Another year, pneumonia, the third a heart attack, bypass surgery and a pacemaker/defibrillator implant. Dad visited the cemetery, driving himself every day until he could no longer drive. After Mom's death, I took Dad to doctors' appointments and we ran errands together. I tried to keep him connected with family and life. His health failed and he lost the will to live and stay engaged. When he could no longer tolerate the pain, he had hip replacement surgery. He ended up having three within four months. I lived with Dad for months until Emily left her life in California to live with him. We thought he was in the dying process in 2010 only to discover he was over-medicated.

To say taking care of Dad was difficult doesn't begin to describe the process. But I had made a promise, a commitment. He instilled in me some of his strength, his sense of duty and honor, and what Emily refers to as "Polish hard-headedness" that I term 'will'. I only recently recognized that my steady knowingness, my calm when others are worried, is the same strong, unwavering faith I saw in Daddy.

Living with constant pain, taking so many medications for so long, took its toll. Dad's liver failed and being unwilling to be hospitalized and not wanting to prolong his life, he entered hospice care.

In the last 20 hours of his life, Daddy woke from sleeping to tell me Mommy was there and they had been having a conversation. I asked if he was in pain and yes he was. After he took his medicine, he asked me not to leave him.

So I held his hand and suggested that Mommy was holding his other hand. I asked if there was anything he needed to say. "I love you" was all he said. I told him that I loved him and was so grateful for everything he had done for me my whole life. I told him that all the kids loved him and were grateful. I was happy Mommy was present. I held his hand until after he fell asleep. I started saying the rosary while he was conscious and continued long after he went to sleep. Daddy never woke up.

I was concerned that his defibrillator would cause him pain when his heart finally stopped. Dad's cardiologist arranged for a tech to come to the house to deactivate it. As his breathing changed, the hospice nurse met the tech at the door. Both Emily and I were at his side, Mommy, too I am sure. We witnessed his last breaths, told him how much we loved him and how grateful we were. His most fervent prayer was finally answered. The Dear Lord took him and he was reunited with his sweetheart.

Love. A mother's love, a father's love, a daughter's love. This is what love looks like for me. I choose to do for others, sometimes out of duty, sometimes because I made a commitment, always because I can and know that what I do will help in some way. Strength, duty, honor, will, faith.

I am grateful for all my parents did for me, their love and support. They showed me ways to live my life. Onto their strong foundation I am adding ways of self care. So the process continues. Each generation builds on what came before, adding to and shifting. I am living the evolution of love.

Karen A. Porter is the author of Live Your Life With Attitude and the Live Your Life With Attitude Workbook/Journal. Now available on Amazon in print and e-book form.

Currently the President of the Board of the non-profit organization Heal My Voice. Karen is a contributing author to all the US HMV books. Karen co-authored Conscious Choices: An Evolutionary Woman's Guide to Life.

Karen is an ordained Minister of Spiritual Peacemaking for the Beloved Community. She practices Sound Massage and leads healing meditations using Tibetan Singing Bowls. Karen is a certified Level 1 Qi Gong Instructor and a Certified Sound Methods Therapist through the American Institute SMT.

Story Twelve

Everything Comes Full Circle

Maryann Hesse

"Find someone to be like and be like them."

Those words echoed in my mind filling me with shame, doubt and tremblings of 'I'm not good enough'. Those words spoken harshly by my mother when I was a young girl colored most of my life to the point that I was always seeking approval from everyone—boyfriends, girlfriends, teachers, employers, neighbors, even strangers. You name it. I was never at ease, always steeling myself against the world, afraid of what someone might say or think about me.

Fast forward to today when my mother has just left the planet after dealing with dementia, and in her final days, a 'brain bleed', and my role as a parent's parent has ended. It's amazing how when things come full circle, everything looks different. The love and compassion I have for her runs really deep. Who would've thought that I could feel this way after years of hating her?

Growing up on the farm, I learned early not to question my elders. It was the 'code' of how we lived in the Midwest. Honor thy father and mother. Always under the hyper vigilant scrutiny of my mother, it was difficult for me to even have a bowel movement unless she was vacuuming and I knew she couldn't hear me. Then I could actually relax my body enough to have a healthy elimination.

My mother went back to teaching school when I started kindergarten. Having my aunt for kindergarten and my mom for first grade was challenging enough, but my mother added additional pressure by informing the entire school staff that if I did anything out of line she was to be notified immediately. To this day I have trouble swallowing pills because in second grade I started choking on a triangular shaped cough drop, and the teacher rushed me down the hall to my mother's classroom while I was still choking. The physical pain in the throat hurt but not nearly as much as the embarrassment and humiliation I felt.

Having been singled out as a teacher's kid, going out for recess gave me a lot of anxiety. Instead of looking forward to playing with other kids, I would spend time being teased and tormented and trying to hide behind a tree or in a corner where no one would notice me.

To make matters worse, we lived outside the school district so I had to ride to school with my mother, and back home again, since no buses ran past our house. Long days intensified by the fact that when we did arrive home, I was not allowed to eat anything with the words "it will spoil your supper". For a growing girl it created headaches and frequent illnesses, and as I've learned as an adult, blood sugar issues.

By seventh grade I got a break from the close daily scrutiny after we relocated and for the first time I rode a bus to school. That didn't end the disdain dished out by my mother though. She was not about to allow me to express myself. In those days 'teasing' your hair and having it be puffed out bouffant style was popular and I was experimenting with setting my hair on rollers and teasing it up. She refused to let me go out of the house "looking like that" and I found that any attempts to express my femininity were simply not acceptable.

When my menstrual cycles began, and my femininity could no longer be denied, she announced this rite of passage into womanhood one night to my Dad at the dinner table; as if it was some sort of action I should be punished for. I was mortified!

At 14, I was actually allowed to go out on a date with a boy in my class. My mother didn't like the idea much, but this time my Dad won out saying he thought it would be okay. I thought that boy was the sun, the moon and the stars. He treated me so nice, complimented me, and affectionately called me 'brown eyes'. He became my whole focus. I was happy for the first time in my life. I woke up thinking about him and went to sleep dreaming about him. I would have done anything for him.

Of course, as with most first loves, it ended after a couple of years. I was devastated. No explanation from him except "he didn't love me anymore". No support at home, in fact my mother accused me of being pregnant because I was worried about gaining weight. Her accusation led to a doctor's office visit to prove to her I wasn't. At that time in my life I didn't know how that was even accomplished, but was also too frightened to speak up for myself, even to the doctor.

This launched my 'love 'em and leave 'em' campaign which lasted most of my adult life. After my marriage ended in shambles, 2 broken engagements--I just couldn't go through with them--and numerous romantic entanglements, I finally just stopped and tried being alone for once in my life.

That didn't actually help much. I could hear my mother's voice at every turn. So I moved to the Southwest and then to California trying to break the 'hold' my mother seemed to have over me. I even changed my name thinking if my name had a different 'resonance' it would help make me a better person. It didn't.

Nothing seemed to ease my inner agony until the day that all my bad habits I had adopted trying to cope with the 'demons in my head'—drinking, drugs, casual sex, excessive exercise, caffeine etc.-- caught up with me and I literally couldn't get out of bed. It was as though the Universe had handed me the check and I had 2 choices: Listen up or Leave the planet.

I chose to listen up and started reading books like "Teachings of the Masters." I began seeking out spiritual teachers, groups, gatherings, events, anything I could find to strengthen my spiritual connection.

Unfortunately, I was still relying on others outside myself for answers. The pattern of turning my power over to others continued. I started studying with a 'spiritual teacher' and being the ever-obedient, good girl, I did everything she told me to do without question. Again, I was not thinking for myself. I started helping out with her family and some of her financial obligations, and an unhealthy relationship 'enmeshment' came about.

Then, she started being plagued by an irrational phobia and looked to me to help her solve her dilemma. I had no clue how to help her but got the idea to stare at a lit candle. Wisdom came forth to me via visions and voices and the information was just what she needed at that time.

This was my first experience of being 'one with the Divine'. I was soon to have many more of these 'wisdom download' experiences as I went through Transformational Prayer Practitioner training.

My life's journey then led me into the jungles of Peru and the highlands of Macchu Picchu. I returned to the States a totally transformed person! The powerful energetic vortexes had intensified the various healing modalities I had been working with. It felt as though I had been transformed at the cellular level. Something major had shifted. I saw everything differently. I was in touch with my body, able to listen and nourish myself in a way that supported my spiritual growth and kept my vibration high. It was then that I began using my hands-on healing abilities to help others.

There were still overtones of negative childhood programming within me that would rear their ugly head from time to time. It wasn't until my mother was diagnosed with dementia, and we began the process of clearing out my childhood home and preparing to sell it, that the deep-seated feelings from my childhood resurfaced, in a way I couldn't deny or run away from.

As we went through the house deciding what to sell, what to keep, and what to give away, I was struck by a lot of different emotions—anger, loss, fear, sadness, occasional spots of 'deLight' and happy feelings. As I unboxed my favorite childhood storybooks, a doll, a tea set...I felt a warmth come over me. Picture albums with photos of me going off to a high school dance in a dress my mother had made for me, brought a new appreciation for my mother, and I began to see the many ways she had tried to express her love for me.

I started asking lots of questions about my relatives, her childhood, and her relationship with my Dad.

Little by little I pieced together the puzzle of who my mother was and what triggered her to behave as she did. I started feeling so much compassion for this woman who had been so fearful all her life, that she locked herself away emotionally, thinking that would keep her safe. And I recognized how **I** had adopted that same way of coping with life! OMG, not easy to admit and come to terms with in myself, yet it opened my heart to her as a fellow wounded female.

As we reminisced, looking through my baby clothes and pictures of me in grade school, college, and married life, I could see the loving hand of my mother in my upbringing and it gave me a new level of understanding of the dynamics between her, my Dad and me.

Looking back over my intimate relationships I could clearly see the patterns that had played out in my own adult life. Not an easy pill to swallow, but it gave me wonderful insights into why my life has taken the twists and turns that it has.

Fortunately it was not too late to create new and more loving experiences with my mother during the last 2 years of her life.

As her only living relative, it was up to me to make decisions about what each next step would be. Assisted living was a great choice for a while, until she started to 'see' people in her living area that weren't physically there and was observed talking to the paper towel rack. Moving her to an Alzheimer's wing was a hard decision, one I really grappled with, yet it provided her with a safer, more closely observed environment. Then after a broken hip and hip replacement, on to a nursing home, until the day she fell and hit her head, causing a skull fracture and brain bleed that ended her life.

During this process I learned a lot about being her advocate. As I stood up and spoke with the nurses, doctors, aides, and administrators of the various facilities for her right to "have her process organically" in this last stage of her life, I felt like her protector, just as she had tried to protect me as a child.

Part of me is really sad that it took my mom's cognitive deterioration for us to begin to heal our relationship and start to become closer. I'm so grateful for the last 2 years that gave me the opportunity, to give back to her the love she was trying to give me all those years, when I had kept her at arm's length, rejecting it and her.

I could see that frightened little girl inside her that had been ruling her life and creating her behavior toward my father and me. I was able to open my heart more and more with every visit and continually surround her energetically with loving energy. I was constantly surprised at how easily and unconditionally my love for her flowed.

There truly IS NOTHING like a Mother's Love and as I recognize more and more the myriad of ways she tried to express her love to me, I'm able to re-write those childhood experiences in my psyche and begin to truly love myself for who I am. As I fully and freely flow love to my mother, wherever she is, and to everyone in my life, I 'get' that love truly IS all there is, and it is everywhere!

My Mom passed just 2 months ago, and as I was going through her belongings and personal items in her desk a couple of days ago, I came across pictures of her as a child and as a teenager that I had never seen before. I was struck with a very deep appreciation for her joyful spirit. These were happy pictures! I don't remember my mother ever laughing. What I wouldn't give to have known her then!

I started feeling regret that I missed having a more fulfilling relationship with her. She seemed to have that with others and I **so** wanted that. Then I realized that with her upbringing and the way her mother had treated her, she was not able to relate to me any differently in this lifetime. I had always kept trying to get something from her that she wasn't able to give! I kept seeing the potential, but it was never realized.

Duh! This is the pattern I had repeated in my romantic relationships—always falling in love with the potential, but it was never able to be realized. No wonder my relationships had never worked out!

Now as I go through the stages of grief, and unpack boxes of memorabilia, I realize that doing my own healing work around these patterns and behaviors, is healing my mother, and her mother, and her mother's mother, and so on through past generations, as the tears flow, as I process, and as I clear out emotional patterns with Shamanic healing, deep breathing, and lots of prayers.

This is my gift of Love to my mother and to my entire ancestry. Everything truly does come full circle and it's never too late.

Love ALWAYS finds a way!

Maryann Hesse *is committed to being a safe place where women naturally relax into who they really are and feel truly seen and heard. As a Women's Empowerment Coach she gently facilitates you to deeper connections with yourself and your loved ones as you take your next steps for your highest evolution. Currently enjoying the single life in Fairfield, Iowa, she can frequently be found at 'live' music events dancing to great blues bands, doing yoga, and communing with nature as she hikes the surrounding trails. Visit her website for a Free Harmonious Relationships Kit at http://www.maryannhesse.com/*

Story Thirteen

Love
Awakening &
Transformation

Nancy Davis

I believe we all have some sort of psychic ability. We just need to tune into it. I believe my "empathic" and "sensitive" abilities surfaced so strongly because I grew up in a family where my father controlled all of us with passive aggressive, verbal abuse. Every evening when he would come home, I would always be on edge not knowing what he was going to say or how my mother, brother, sister or I would be treated. I learned to "sense or feel" his mood and tune in to how the evening or weekend would go.

Even at a young age I tried to focus on the things I'm interested in, instead of the negativity in the house. I spent most of my time listening to music and dreaming about and researching the mysteries of the World; Machu Picchu, the Paranormal, angels, psychic ability, crypto zoology, just to name a few. I started to watch the hit show "In Search Of" with Leonard Nimoy when I was seven years old. Travel, the unexplained and personal potential have always intrigued me. It was a great escape to focus on topics of interest that were more important to me than the chaos in my childhood home.

In 1997, my father passed away from a major heart attack at the age of 50. I believe that his anger, verbal abuse and inability to love was part of his early death and he was also an unhealthy eater. He only ate meat and potatoes and would laugh at us if anyone was trying to change their food plan, or to improve themselves in any way.

When he died my mother was unable to take care of herself. My father had controlled her during their entire marriage and forced her to be a stay at home mom with no skills and no college education. His belittling of her left her with no self-confidence to take care of herself. My mother went into a deep depression and became ill with horrible diseases like diabetes, diabetic retinopathy (now legally blind), total kidney failure and with the need for dialysis three days per week. She suffers from high blood pressure, congestive heart failure and more.

Within 5 years of my father's death, my mother had blown through all of the money my father left for her. She was going to have to sell her house and had nowhere left to go. I made the mistake of saying to her one night that she could move in with us and that I would always make sure that she was taken care of. This escalated her going into an even deeper depression. She refused to take care of herself. She refused to give herself injections or to check her blood sugar and she expected me to do it for her. I did take care of her because I loved her and didn't want to see her get any worse and it was frustrating that she wouldn't take care of things that she was capable of doing.

For about two years, I would only go to work, come home and take care of her and my two children. I was barely able to leave the house and was completely exhausted. I was sick all of the time and didn't know why. I was taking on all of her negative energy and still housing my father's negativity and inability to love and it was making me sick. I am not a nurse and my mother should have been living in an assisted living facility.

One of the hardest things about my relationship with my mother was remembering who she was in the past and continuing to love and care for her. She is someone who used to be funny, full of life and spunk. Now, I am seeing her morph and change into someone I don't know. It was like I was dealing with a pod person who stopped taking responsibility for her life. She is now just the shell of the mother who raised me from child to adult. I remember the good times of singing the Bee Gees with her while driving in her 70's van and playing Frisbee. Now she has kidney failure and is in complete denial sitting on my couch reeking of urine.. I finally looked at her one day and said, "Are you going to die here on my couch or are you going to go and have the port put into your shoulder so you can start having dialysis? The choice is yours." She agreed that afternoon to get it done.

The situation continued to get even worse. By Christmas night of 2010 she was creating more drama of needing attention and wanting me to take her to the Emergency room because her nose was stuffed up. I looked at her and said, "I'll take you and drop you off at the door. I'm not sitting in the waiting room with all of those germs and sick people. I can't help you, only the nurses and doctors can. When you're done, you call me and I will come and pick you up."

We got in my car, it was sleeting and the roads were bad. I dropped her off and my brother picked her up and brought her back to my house. She was angry because I wouldn't sit there with her. It was time for tough love. I couldn't sacrifice my health and my children anymore. I looked at her and said, "I love myself too much to continue living this way. I love my kids too much to be putting myself through this. I can't do this anymore." About 5 months later, she went away for a couple of days and we cleaned and threw away some of the things she had all over the house. It was everywhere!

My action of self-love created forward movement. My mother purchased her own apartment and moved out. I'm still working on forgiveness and healing. Our relationship is still strained. It has been two years now and I have only seen and talked to her a little more than a handful of times. The last time I saw her we ended up talking about gardening the entire time. She used to love planting flowers, herbs and vegetable gardens. It was nice to see her light up when we were chatting about it. I've come to understand that this is her path and that I cannot make her want to live. I have come to understand that love really is what life is all about and I continue to heal within myself.

It is kind of funny and ironic that that was the conversation we had. Our love of gardening. When my mother was still living with me and we were in the middle of all of this craziness, I decided to take my kids to the National Zoo in DC on a summer afternoon. We drove in since they have parking at the zoo, but the parking lot was full. I thought oh well, we'll just go home. While driving home, a thought came to me to stop at The National Arboretum. So, I said, "Okay"! I pulled in and they had plenty of parking. I had been using herbs and reading and studying about them for a long time. So funny that although I had not visited the arboretum in about 12 years the first sign I saw read, "National Herb Garden." I was blown away that I had been led here that day and that the largest herb garden in the United States is less than 30 minutes from my house. I was running from garden to garden with a big smile on my face, checking out everything from basil to hot peppers and loving every minute of it. That night I emailed my best friend about my experience. She was like, "Duh! Why don't you volunteer there and give tours. You're so into gardening and herbs already". This was not obvious to me at first and then I said,, "Duh! You're right"!

So within 9 months or so of visiting the arboretum, my mother had moved out, my job of 15 years had been eliminated and I contacted the arboretum. They welcomed me with open arms and I have been volunteering in the Herb Garden now for two years. It has been a huge healing force in my life and I am so grateful for this hands-on experience.

My coach and friend said something to me that hit me deeply about two years ago. She said, "You don't love yourself very much do you"? I felt that. Ever since that day, I make sure that I am loving myself and that I do loving things for me. I enjoy gardening, listening to music, reading, traveling, and taking time to give myself the best self-care I can give.

Through my process of loving myself and setting boundaries of love, I have been able to forgive my mother and father for their behavior. I have come to understand that they were doing the best they could. I don't think my father had any idea how he affected those around him and that he did not love himself. Looking back, would I change my childhood? I've come to the tough answer of no. I've learned to embrace what I have been through. After watching my father pass away and my mother suffer so horrifically I made the choice to seek out a healthier path for my life; body, mind and soul. It has all made me who I am today and I believe that I can help others with how I have been able to heal. I have moved on to the life I was meant to live.

The quote, "Be the change you wish to see in the world" is so true. The change starts within each of us.. Consciously treating others with respect, love and wishing them the best. Noticing what is in their highest good and taking action has brought the same energy back to me. Everyday I read high vibrational quotes and writings help me maintain a high level of vibrational thoughts of hope, love and compassion. I guide my children consciously to find their mission in life and encourage their interests and strengths so they can live a happy and meaningful life of purpose.

I love myself more and more and in doing so I feel better and better each day. I have connected and become friends with some absolutely amazing people around the world and I am so grateful and blessed. I am so in love with life and the unlimited possibilities that are waiting for me and for everyone who chooses to know what they can accomplish. Surrounding yourself with what brings you unending joy and loving yourself is definitely the key.

Nancy Davis is a big advocate for organic gardening and natural healing. She believes in growing food not lawns. Herbal medicine and a vast amount of alternative healing methods have helped her to transform her life from what it once was to what it is today. She lives in southern Maryland with her family. Nancy currently works in the travel industry. In her spare time she volunteers at the local arboretum in their herb garden and visits local botanical gardens for inspiration. Her goal is to run her own organic farm.

Section Four

I AM Big-Hearted

Our senses are indeed our doors and windows on this world, in a very real sense the key to the unlocking of meaning and the wellspring of creativity.

~Jean Houston

Story Fourteen

Dancing with the Wind to Carry Me Home to Myself

Kathleen Ann Marye

Me. A young child.

The light was streaming into the toy room of my parents home in New Hampshire. My mother was upstairs in the kitchen and my two siblings were playing outside. I was alone singing and dancing to the music I was making on my little, orange, plastic flute. A beautiful golden light was streaming through the window and onto my toy box. I turned around and standing before me was a very tall, Native American man with long, black hair and amazing green blue eyes. He wore no shoes just jeans and a flannel blue shirt. Even back then I thought, "Who is he? He's cute."

The first thing he spoke to me was, "Please don't be afraid. I won't hurt you. I'm here to ask a question. Do you mind?" I said okay because I felt in my heart, he was special. I could feel his beautiful loving heart and see the light behind his eyes. It was different from my siblings or my parents. I said, "Okay. My name is Kathleen. What do you want to ask?" He said, "What would you love to do when you grow up, dear one?"

"I would love to sing, dance and bring peace and I really love playing my flute. I always want to play my flute." He said something like, "I must go now. I love you. I will return one day." I wanted to give him a hug but he had disappeared. I checked all the other rooms with a puzzled, confused feeling. Mom came downstairs. She asked, "Didn't you hear me calling you?" I said, "No, I was talking to the man. He was very nice." Mom didn't understand what I was talking about.

****

In the last fifteen years, my life drastically changed. I had a variety of health issues, including asthma and feelings of not being good enough, having no voice, body issues, environmental sensitivities and stressors. I also had to be concerned with seeing things that no one else saw. I had no one to open to discuss and ask, "What the hell is going on?"

I went into a full-blown psychosis in 1998 for 4 months and had a seizure from another medication. It felt like I was slammed into the mental ward and "prison" of Franklin Square Hospital where they labeled me as bipolar. The doctors did not offer me an explanation of what was going on. During that time, I felt like I was picking up on energy and feeling people who had died in my room. I was spiritually feeling stuff and it was labeled as illness. It has been difficult to have people see me as ill rather than see what a beautiful spirit I am.

When I was thrown into my first quiet room with only a blue mat on the floor, I cried from the depths of my soul to be heard by my closest Archangels and my guardian angel, Abbygale. I cried out, "Please, I've done nothing wrong. Why am I here? Michael, I'm scared. What did I do? Don't allow me to forget who I am. Allow me to remember, Abbygale. Hear me, Michael." I pleaded in tears to be heard and seen. I didn't understand and no one helped me to understand what was going on. I wanted to die because I felt abandoned. I was left in a place I didn't recognize or understand. I just wanted to go home.

When the staff let me out of the quiet room, the only way I felt I could be clean from what I was picking up on energetically was to take baths and showers. I didn't know how to express what I was feeling and I was afraid I would get locked up again. Doctors gave me toxic drugs like Lithium and Depakote and I felt like I was in a time shift.

Everything is so mixed up from that time. I believed I was experiencing an allergic reaction to the other drug. There was so much stress in my home environment and I was in a spiritual awakening. I had a greater purpose and I had to choose to love myself first. I wanted to teach people to learn to walk in another person's moccasins, to choose love and to remember that we are all unique. It is through love that we can heal all obstacles and soar again.

Despite all my health challenges I didn't give up. I decided to strive to become my best self, to take my power back and allow myself to be heard in everything. I decided to choose love.

My dreams have been crushed more than once. After graduating from Kutztown University, I had a dream to play in a symphony as a master flutist. Even when my private teacher told me I'd never be good enough to play in an orchestra, I kept making music from my heart and I came to love every instrument I touched. I decided to do it my way so when I share my music from my heart. I love uplifting others from my wind and my art.

I may not know all of the steps to where I am going. I do know I am always guided with my intuition. I was given advice from my soul brother, Austin, who taught me to know that Spirit always guides me and keeps me safe. I just need to relax and trust. He encouraged me back in August 2012 to join a survivor's group and see what's out there. I did that and I was given the opportunity to go to Colorado in September 2012 with First Descents…

I rode a plane for the first time ever on Southwest Airlines! I decided to have fun. I said yes this is for me and for me alone. I met amazing new friends and the land accepted me home. I'm Blackfoot Cherokee and Creek Native American and I'm very connected to the land. Before I left, Austin gave me a tiny traveling Native American flute to be able to play and share my music. I was happy the whole week and accepted by total strangers. I rose above the physical challenges of asthma, my weight and I got over my fear of heights.

I was gifted in many ways by spirit. Each morning I awoke early before breakfast. I walked away from the house to explore, to walk with spirit and play my flute. On the third day, I walked out to the furthest hill, found a place by a cedar tree, offered some shaman coffee as a thank you and spoke prayers cried in thanks as I played my flute. As I walked up the hill to where I would sit on the rock by the cedar tree, I spooked a golden eagle in a nest and it flew away screeching. I played music for the tree spirits and possibly young eagles in the nest. During my climbs the rest of the week, I was blessed to see golden eagles every day. One eagle hovered only 25 feet above me while I was dipping my feet in the cool clear water of a huge lake. This golden eagle was gorgeous with flecks of gold auburn coloring on the feathers. When I felt a knowing that it was time to go back to climbing I said thank you and the golden eagle left.

On the last day, with everyone who was to travel to the airport with me, we witnessed a golden eagle fly over our van. It screeched three times. I was so sad to leave. I whispered thank you to the eagle and said I would return to Colorado to come home again.

Flash forward to the week before KarmaFest in May 2013. I decided to step out and share my intuitive teacher role. I played my flute and beautiful music poured through me and to the people at the Festival.

I'm choosing a different perspective now. I put myself in everyone's shoes to love and accept them. I am thankful for what I have learned. People are people and what we choose to see is only half the journey. It's how we choose to keep going and uplifting each other in any given moment that is important. I'm looking at what I can do and how I can listen to my heart. I can choose love or fear. I'm choosing to walk a path of love because of all of my experiences.

What I want more than anything is to write and play music and sing and dance. In life, we come home not only to ourselves, we come full circle to our dreams of becoming the music of our soul. Being a musician, a flute player and whatever else I desire can happen in the blink of a moment. I can choose to follow my heart even when I'm not sure of my footsteps. I walk through my fears and move through life with love, singing and dancing and being my beautiful soul self. I uplift others through the music that moves through me to all those around me. I give voice to the seen and unseen in this world. I walk with my heart as my guiding light and I trust that my angels and god take care of the rest to guide me on the wind home.

Thank you for hearing my voice and saying yes to dancing with the wind of love and transformation.

Kathleen Ann Marye is a compassionate, fun dynamic, loving Spiritual Teacher/ Intuitive Advisor who is certified as a Kundalini Reiki Master Healer. As a spiritual teacher and healer of other indigos like herself, she shares her wealth of knowledge and gifts openly to those who will listen. It's her wish to live in Eugene, Oregon to open a sanctuary for other light workers to come learn in mini workshops and receive reiki offerings & meditations. Email at rainbowhawkcloud@yahoo.com for any further inquiries (i' d love to hear from you! blessings Kathleen)

Story Fifteen

Surviving Is Not Enough: And so I go on...

Jamie Dee Schiffer

This is not the story I had planned to write. When I set out on this journey ~ writing about love ~ my intent was to share my experience of unconditional love, of being wholly loved and not just accepted, but cherished... of loving my soulmate. I thought that I could interject bits of wisdom about being a loving force in the world, about seeing all things and all people through the eyes of love. That was going to be a beautiful story. A happy story. A joy-filled story.

The Universe, however, had different plans.

Despite some major odds that my soulmate and I faced, I always believed that we would find our way, that we could be together and live a life of total bliss. I am now coming to terms with the notion that my dream may not come to fruition in this lifetime.

As I've lost myself in the grief of this overwhelming loss, the depths of the despair that I've felt have triggered memories from my past...memories that I had completely repressed...ones that I had no conscious awareness of until the flashbacks started.

Flashbacks. I had no real idea what this word actually meant until I experienced them. I'd always imagined them to simply be a flash back in time, a vivid memory. I've always had an amazing memory and have been able to recall the smallest of details from past events. I had no idea that a true flashback made you feel as though you were literally in that event – every sight, sound, taste, touch, emotion – as if you were right there again, in that moment, RIGHT THEN.

The flashbacks started occurring everywhere; standing in the aisle of the grocery store, driving down the highway, in the middle of conversations with other people. It didn't matter where I was, or what I was doing I couldn't escape. I was "there", trapped in those moments that took place over 25 years ago. I was drugged in a bar and brutally raped by two men who left me for dead on a street corner... there are still huge gaps of missing time and details, but what I do remember of the attack is enough to give anyone nightmares for a lifetime.

My therapist thinks that I'm suffering from Post-Traumatic Stress Disorder (PTSD) and that the depth of my grief and sorrow over the loss of my soulmate has triggered these deep, dark, buried memories. I have evidently never expressed such depth of emotion, preferring instead to keep a huge wall between myself and any potential pain. I was aware of my wall, but didn't know the "Why" behind its existence. I always just thought I was being shrewd and pragmatic in my approach to relationships – painfully logical.

"If you don't want me, well then FUCK YOU, that's your loss." Very mature, I know, but it protected me from truly feeling the loss over two failed marriages.

As I go through therapy and attempt to lessen the debilitating effects of the flashbacks, I've found a deep need to understand all of this from a spiritual standpoint as well. I'm not talking about the bemoaning question "Why Me", but the bigger "Why" in what soul lesson am I supposed to learn from this experience.

I've tried to wrap my brain around the smaller question of "why now?". Why, when I'm already suffering so much, would spirit push me further and pull the foundation out from under me. How can I possibly hold it all together, function "normally" when my mind is in a constant spiral? How can I deal with these flashbacks when the only truly safe place that I've ever known is in the arms of my soulmate, and he is no longer there to protect me, to support me, to guide me?

My spiritual counselor tells me that this is happening NOW because I'm ready for it, ready and capable of handling these truths after all this time. I can't quite tell if she truly believes that, or just desperately wants ME to believe it. I doubt that truth, and my own abilities to cope on a daily basis. I put on a brave face and go out into the world, pretending to be OK. I'm often surprised by those who believe it. I'm more surprised by those who can see past the mask. I'm so afraid to reveal the truth of my fragile state to anyone. I mean, I'm supposed to be "the strong one", the leader, the one with answers, the one everyone else leans on when they need help. How can I be all of that and be this weak, frail victim?

God, I hate that word – victim. An incredibly strong woman that I know from another book circle told me that I'm a survivor. I don't own that title yet. Not today. Today I am caught in the pain, the embarrassment, the guilt, the loss, the anger, the sorrow. Today I am swirling in doubt that I can go on, that I even want to go on.

I really thought that I had conquered all of my demons. I've done years of "shadow work" dealing with the darker side of my self – those not so nice aspects of my personality that out of fear, or a sense of lack, lashed out at others, said mean and nasty things. There is no pride to be found in realizing what a mean and heartless bitch you've been at certain points along your path. I've offered many heartfelt apologies and truly thought I'd done the work to forgive others, and the even more difficult work of forgiving myself. A solid 7 years of very focused and intensive spiritual study, immersion and work to come to an understanding and acceptance of who I am and what my purpose is in this lifetime.

The revelations have been flooding my consciousness on a daily basis since the flashbacks started. I now find myself swimming in a sea of sadness as I look back on my supposed "over-reactions" to the simplest of perceived wrongdoings; the shooting pain and obvious flinches that occurred when being hugged by my then-husband. They all take on a new and deeper meaning in light of this freshly opened wound. It pains me now to think of how I pushed him away during my desperate attempts to protect myself. He was right when he said that I wasn't capable of forgiving, but what neither of us realized was that it wasn't just about him. I was incapable of forgiving the men who had stripped me of my ability to trust ANYONE.

It's not that I wasn't able to give. There are many who could tell you that I gave more than anyone they knew. I just couldn't receive. I couldn't (can't?) trust that someone is not going to hurt me at some point, and so I wrap myself in protective layers of defensiveness and "over-sensitivity" that build the walls in which I live. The slightest pain, emotional or physical, caused me to push away, and not just a little bit... completely. I'd rather be alone. My ex always said that I didn't NEED anyone. I used to take great pride in that. I thought that meant that I was strong, independent, and free-spirited.

Deeper exploration of the "Why" I can't trust is revealing that underneath this strong armor lies the pervasive belief that I am ultimately not worthy of being loved, that I am disposable, just like those men disposed of me on a street corner in Philly after they had used me for their own entertainment. There is a part of me who still believes that despite all that I do, all that I give... it's never enough, and that eventually I will be discarded.

I believe SOOO strongly in the value, the worth, the equality of ALL living things... I've fought for, counseled, and championed others when their own belief had failed them. How many times have I said the words "fear and faith cannot co-exist" to others? How many times have I explained to my friends, my clients, my acquaintances, that simply their existence as a child of God, of the Universe, that they are divinely loved and worthy of receiving all the good in the world. My sad, dark, dirty little secret is that even though I say the words, there is still a scared young woman inside of me who doesn't believe that of herself.

And now I find myself questioning that even through the experience of the love of my soulmate, the feeling of unconditional love and acceptance, did I push him away too? Did my fear of rejection, the deep disbelief that I deserved his love, did I end it all because underneath everything, it was ME who didn't believe that I was worth fighting for, worth waiting for?

I hear myself answer with the ever-so-polite "I'm fine" when asked how I am, but inside I'm screaming "LIAR! You're NOT fine, you're anything BUT fine!" It's painful to realize how few people actually want to know the REAL answer to that question. I die inside a little every time I force myself to put on my mask and pretend to be okay just so that I don't make others uncomfortable with my truth. There are so many days where all I want to do is crawl under the covers and never come out. Sometimes all that I can think about are all the things I've done wrong, all the things I could have done better, had I only been aware of the reason why I was so closed off, so guarded and defensive.

It's been said that the easiest and best way to lift yourself is to lift others. I find myself searching out ways to do something good, something meaningful. I've seriously entertained the idea of living in a monastery, becoming a missionary, or signing up do something/anything in which I give up all of my worldly possessions and focus solely on the good of others. I've been looked at as though I were crazy. Hell, some people have told me straight out they think I am. But they don't know, they don't understand.

Many people can't seem to wrap their minds around the notion that I have absolute zero interest in getting involved with another man, in "finding love" and getting married again. A few have even taken extreme measures and tried to ambush me into a fix-up date. I try to remind myself that they are doing this out of love and concern for me, that in their minds, I deserve to be loved and therefore "should" be in a relationship. I feel badly for those poor men who must have been severely coerced into believing that meeting me was a good idea. Lord only knows what they said after I left, but I do hope that I made it clear that it was not about them – George Clooney himself wouldn't stand a chance of wooing me right now.

Yes, in case you're wondering, I'm aware that I'm building another wall. But where I am now, I need it. I need to feel safe. I also need to feel that what I'm doing in this lifetime is worthwhile, that I'm worthwhile. I don't see the harm in pursuing my passion of healing and helping others. I have my son to think about as well. He'll be off to college faster than I can blink an eye, and I want to be fully present for him, for all of his challenges and his triumphs. I can't be lost in a swirling mess of depression over what I've lost, what I've endured, on any level. We ALL have our stories, our pain, and I'm even more aware and sensitive now than ever to the journey of others. I HAVE to pick myself back up and learn to function again, to not just survive, but to thrive. Finding appreciation and gratitude in the small things keeps me grounded in the here and now. Focusing on work that can bring me joy and fulfillment keeps me hopeful about the future. I know that I still have a LOT of personal work to do, a tremendous amount of healing needs to happen before I can fully embrace life again.

Little by little, day-by-day with the help of many amazing, loving and supportive people, I Will find my way. I Will continue to search out all of those scared, dark, lonely places inside of me and find a way to touch them with love because that is what we survivors do. We go on.

Jamie Dee is blessed to be a mom to her amazing son, Logan who provides endless laughter, light and inspiration. She is a relationship communication educator, coach, author, speaker and workshop leader. Jamie is a non-denominational minister who loves creating beautiful, customized vows & performing wedding ceremonies. As a dual doctoral candidate in psychology & theology, and years of being a dedicated Heart-Centered Metaphysician, Jamie provides a positive, nurturing support system that allows her clients to grow & reach their full potential. Jamie is a Life Coach who offers extensive PreMarital Counseling & Marriage Enrichment packages as well as gentle guidance on how to have a graceful divorce & move forward with life through her Divorce Coaching program and in her soon to be released book, "A Graceful Divorce; Learning How to Communicate with Integrity, Respect & Honor".

You can reach Jamie at the following: www.A-Passionate-Life.com

Story Sixteen

Reclaiming Myself, Kicking, "The Habit"

Brenda Jacobi

Gone was my pride! Drown in a sea of tears that wouldn't fall. A most sacred and cherished part of me dead! What I wanted, dreamed of, cherished and imagined as an occasion of pure joy, ecstasy, beauty, radiance and bliss turned into a scene from Disney's, *The Little Mermaid* where Ariel exchanged her beautiful voice for human legs. Ariel's deal was with Ursula, the Sea Witch and mine with God who was just as mean, ugly and cruel! Even worse because I was taught God was love and this wasn't love though God, Himself seemed to want me to comply!

It didn't matter how many times I protested. My potential fiancé would only marry a woman he had sex with first, before we got married. I overrode my body's repulsion. I steeled my nerves. He wanted a submissive wife and I had been taught to be dutiful my whole life. Why couldn't he see that? Not like this. No! While my emotions were shattered physically I felt nothing at all.

He had been my aunt and uncle's foster son and had remained in touch with them throughout the years. He returned home from the Army and began to pay attention to me though there was no physical affection at first. He wanted a wife who was strong and would never betray him. One who would bear his children and raise them with the physical affection and support he did not know himself; A wife who would also support him in his quest to become a medical physician. I could do that easily. It was a piece of cake as long as he would one day financially support me, and the children we would have together.

I was not the first woman he sought to marry, nor the first to conceive his child. I was simply the one who believed his dream would come true. I believed in him and I had the courage and conviction to see him through what medical school would demand. I would start a family with him and be devoted. I ignored my feelings even though he was not the man I originally wanted to marry either. (I kept that hidden) He was not the kind of man I could speak such truth to and expect to be treated with kindness or respect. No, I was most certain he would be as harsh and judgmental as my father.

We were both raised Catholic. Though he was not practicing, we both wanted a Catholic wedding and to raise our family in the faith. We knew the teachings. We were a proud people! Especially, of our Holy Catholic Church: *The One True Faith*. While I didn't like our rules, I was a seeker and sought to follow them and bring order to my life. Certainly, one day I would figure them out even though they didn't make any sense and seemed to change according to circumstance.. I preferred fairy tale romance where life made sense with order and happy endings! Bible stories could be perilous and made me feel sad and filled me with fear, doubt and confusion! Many of them seemed downright cruel though I was told they were *love*!

A good Catholic knew that this wasn't love and that eventually you would have to repent. I figured that is why God put us together. Until that day he would have me and sin no more. The only problem was that now I had to sin in the most hideous of ways. Why did they both want me to betray myself and call it love? How could that be appealing to anyone?

I longed for attention and affection. I wanted to know the freedom of a "hippie" "flower child" person that I had seen on television in my youth. In my family and church these people were presented as enemies of God. I was told to be wary of them as they practiced *free* sex, drugs and rock n' roll! I loved some rock n' roll and I couldn't imagine not liking sex! What captivated me most about them was their sense of connection to the earth and Mother Nature. They seemed in tune in a more natural way. I imagined them to be similar to the Indians and gypsies of the past whom I admired from afar. They seemed truly peace filled and at rest with God and Mother Nature. How could their peace be opposing God and His will? They had courage and the gall to oppose religion, politics, war and government!

My father was active military set to retire. He had fought in the Vietnam War. He was a knight in *Our Holy Catholic Church* though often not valiant and rarely what I would call saintly! Seldom did I see a look of peace or joy wash over or through him. He and my mother fought incessantly! He was an alcoholic though drinking wasn't his only problem. Anger was. It drove him to acts of violence and rage! My mother's response was to shy away in fear, worry and deceit in her attempt to create a sense of ease, normalcy and calm.

When I was five, I wanted to be like Nancy Sinatra who was bold and beautiful! Her boots were made for walkin'. Though according to my father she would be walkin' straight to hell for being a fornicator! No one refuted or disputed my father's claims. Did that mean I would be going to hell too? I felt sexy, powerful, beautiful, free and fun when I wore my white go-go boots or high-heeled red clogs with the cork sole that I picked out myself! I was just glad that no one seemed to notice. I figured on account of my age they weren't really looking. This afforded me time before I would have to alienate myself from what felt like beauty, grace and love. These were only my feelings. They weren't supposed to matter!

Once I was certain of this man's interest in me I was in constant search as to how I could respect a man who cared more that he got "sex" then that he loved me! His kisses felt contrived as a ploy for sex. They were void of emotion and an attempt to connect with me. I felt as though his only purpose was to devour and conquer me as his own spoil of war to make a trophy as opposed to a cherished guest of honor! I wanted to engage in play and he went straight for sex regardless of how I pulled away, told him, "No." and sought to distract him. He seemed only encouraged by my resistance. Normally, I made no such exceptions though God was full of exceptions and I figured he was asking me to be, too. So. I slept with him not wanting to all the way!

Looking back I can see how I spent much of my marriage seeking to know how he loved me in a fashion that measured up to the love I had known as a teenager . I wanted our love to be new or different from how he had ever loved another before me. When I took the lead he had no idea how to follow. When he almost begged me to take the lead, he still didn't follow even when all of the pleasure and love was pointed at him. I felt as though my loving him was viewed as competition that he sought to squash. When I asked him to speak to me his reply was that he liked it silent. I gave him quiet after that. I became so quiet even a deaf man could hear me scream!

While I wanted sex in our marriage what I wanted more than anything was to make love to this man, the father of my children, the man with whom I was spending my life! The words *make love* never escaped his mouth. He only ever used the word "sex". My children were my only sense of our shared sacred and when a wedge was driven there I felt defeated! I knew what was possible and should he never speak to me with words I wanted to hear and held dear how could we ever bridge this gap? I wanted to feel special, appreciated and valued! His touch did not convey these feelings to me and the message I received when he told me he loved me was with the tone , "Don't ever leave me.". I rarely told him I loved him. Even though I loved him my tone could only imply I was not in love with him.

I didn't need intercourse to have an orgasm of the heart. I needed freedom, connection, trust and respect! There was a moment after 12 years of marriage when he finally agreed to pray with me. How I had been craving this with all my heart, soul and prayers! And while his words were offensive I could hear the sincerity and love with which he meant them and a connection began to forge. He was open and receptive to what I would call the Holy Spirit and for the first time ever our breaths began to sync as one! His next words continued the disappointment as he professed he would never pray with me again...

With all of his previous sexual experience and book knowledge of which he was so proud how could he not know where this was headed? Or did he and he was just as scared? Would we be profound or profane? Would he continue to be the ogre I once saw in him or was he now more like Shrek? Would he be my prince charming? And I, Fiona? Though stuck in what form? No longer did I have claim to my youth filled virtues of my Cinderella past once filled with beauty, grace and tact! We had been ingrained in our habit.

Once again, the Holy Spirit visited upon us. I could feel this opening and opportunity with the familiar energy of lovers present among us and I dare say he made an attempt at flirting with me! While I very much wanted to encourage his behavior I had no idea how! How do I blot out and ignore the all too familiar look of hurt, rejection and pain that flashed within his eyes as though he had already decided, "Why bother!" For me this was a turning point! An opportunity for him to follow through with his own suggestion of love for us! He would have been loving me and simultaneously himself! We could have been naughty and nice! No betrayal, shame, anger, fear, guilt or rejection.

Years of anguish could be washed away with this single gesture of love! Finally we would be living the life of our dreams as he was finally willing to spend his hard earned cash and time on me! I would be the only recipient of his love. We could have fun! Nothing contrived, premeditated or thought out. Everything had already been taken care of. The kids were being tended to and all we had to do was tend to ourselves. We could be more than roommates or parents! We could be ourselves being both friends and lovers. I didn't know how to affirm for him what I already knew in my heart that all our years of hard work pain and anguish could be gently laid to rest and washed away! This would be our life now! We had finally succeeded in creating our dream! The one we had both fought and struggled so hard to achieve, preserve and protect from even ourselves. We had arrived!

Not knowing my place in my life or his I once again allowed him to take the lead. He cancelled his brilliant suggestion that we have lunch and get a room in the prominent upscale hotel where we ate a fine lunch that neither of us enjoyed. All I could think of was the fun we weren't having in a room above our heads. I wanted nothing more than to be intimate with this man, my husband!. Instead, we parted and went our separate ways. I went back to tending our children while he played golf.

In our earlier years we had little money and his time was mostly accounted for leaving little with me. He entrusted our finances and children to me as these were my strong suits (while I also worked). I had full charge though I needed to account to him which meant getting us out of debt and keeping us that way. As our livelihood increased and grew sizably so did his many interests and activities along with how he spent money. He afforded himself far more freedom than he applied to me as he took over the responsibility of our family finances. It was still my job to scrimp and save so that he could splurge where he saw fit. He gave us nice things though not necessarily what we would prefer. I had no desire to be oppressed by stuff and activities. My life was full of obligations. I wanted a partner.

I began to see that his sense of loyalty was to his own pursuits of power and fun, which became more evident regardless of how I tried to stop our fighting. We were at war. While I didn't want divorce I wanted freedom for both him and myself and to end the power trips and sexual oppression for ourselves and our children. I wanted him to uphold the love he claimed to have for me, our family and our faith. Being ever dutiful to him and our religion I sought to grant him an annulment so he could freely choose me and our family with no strings attached because finally I found the courage to tell him of my secret that I had harbored in my heart now finally confirmed within me that love is was what I had once been in prior to knowing him. I knew the foundation of our marriage would concede to the rigors of Church law for these findings.

The problem was the Church would not grant an annulment without first transacting a legal divorce. That is a story for another day.

After 20 years, six kids and not a single orgasm of my own, I divorced him, I could struggle no more to find a common bond for a shared sense of the sacred between us.

While I still have my moments and there has been much pain, hurt and sorrow my heart is reopening. Post divorce I have still grieved for what never was and what I have wanted and what has felt like the loss of my family and personal identity. Some days the paradox of the contrast between what my heart experiences as precious, true and dear when compared to the circumstances of my life feels like more than I can bear. And yet, I venture forward being the mental gymnast in my epic life adventure as I become both flexible and strong, as I merge my masculinity with my femininity, as I harmonize and resurrect who I am. Regardless of where I have been, what I have done, not done and who I have been. Some days I haven't known if the pain and sorrow within me would ever end. I have felt as though death may be my only answer yet death to what as my body is so filled with life? Or is life more of a process of revealing that allows all to come into being? I can no longer bottle up my feelings holding them inside as though they are meaningless. Both are worthy of expression. They do not make me bad or good. They make me human and help me navigate my journey as I claim my life, love, beauty and sexuality.

I no longer look to Mother Church to tell me the answers for my life and reclaim my power from religion and the God I was taught to fear!

I choose life. I choose love.

I am peace. I am prosperity. I am joy. I am freedom.

I am love.

*Hi, I'm **Brenda Jacobi**, my passions and interests are as varied as my eclectic gypsy spirit! You may find me leading a drum circle, dancing Nia, doing Forrest Yoga, fertility coaching or cleaning homes. I love the feel of a good (non-toxic) clean home with results that are immediate though not as lasting as a child. I especially enjoy being appreciated and tipped when people are especially grateful for the difference I make in their lives and world! What lights you up? Should you like to contact me you can reach me:*

*@ **Brenda.jacobi@gmail.com** or find me on Facebook. I live in Portland, OR.*

Story Seventeen

Living the Love of the Universe...
And other confessions from the
woowoo side of life

AnnaMariah Nau

I want to start this off with a declaration of intent. My purpose is to *Live the Love of the Universe on Earth.* Okay, there, I've said it. I'm shaking, but it's out there, up front, no wavering, just my truth as it stands.

That may not seem like a big deal, or maybe it just sounds crazy to you. I don't know, but let's take this back a step.

I have a confession to make. Back in the early 90's I was

one of those new-agey flakey types that make me cringe and roll my eyes today. I didn't run around with fairy wings or anything like that, but I did do a lot of pretty weird woowoo stuff. Let me explain before you think I'm completely nuts.

I was a deeply mystical child with a sense of magic and purpose. I wanted to be a nun. Anyone who knows me now thinks that statement is completely unbelievable and even shocking. I'm an outside-the-box, irreverent, rule breaker with an infectious laugh, definitely *Not* nun material. But at that time, I didn't know any other way to live a spiritual life.

When I was twelve, as a Catholic I was excited to be receiving the sacrament of Confirmation. There was a huge build-up about how differently I would feel afterwards. The big day came. I trembled with anticipation. I'd read stories of saints who had wept with the bliss of their connection to god. I wanted to feel that.

Alas, that was not to be. During the service the Monsignor stated, "The way to god is through fear." My world stopped. Everything in me recoiled. "That simply couldn't be true. Wasn't it through love?" I pushed that thought away and gave myself up to the ceremony, trusting that I would feel something by the end. Nothing. Just nothing. In that moment I knew, "The Church *didn't* know." I wasn't sure what it was they didn't know. I knew for certain that they did not know the thing that was most important – whatever that was.

I used to watch the nuns walk and pray in the gardens and I felt their peace. I wanted, expected to feel that same peace and devotion. Such a small part of their lives, but something I longed for deep in my soul. Discovering that the answer wasn't there for me was shattering beyond belief.

A part of me died. I dropped out of anything that looked remotely religious, any system that preached fear was just wrong! I had no understanding that there was a spirituality that existed beyond the trappings of religion. I was bereft.

I won't go through the struggles I went through during the following twenty-five years; I was cut off from an essential part of myself. Something was missing. Don't get me wrong, I wasn't miserable – but I knew I wasn't fully something. I wasn't sure what I wasn't but it was something I longed for, ached for.

In 1989, at the age of 37, I had a dream, a mystical experience that reawakened my soul. Shortly afterwards I discovered new age spiritualism in a book on past lives that my aunt had left behind. It made sense. Then, surprisingly, through reading tarot cards I tapped into another level of spirituality and I felt *right* somehow.

I became obsessed with filling myself up with all that I'd missed. I'd been reborn. I grinned for no reason at all. I'd found god/goddess/the universe/all-that-is-in a very personal way that I could literally feel and communicate with. I jumped into the deep waters of new-agism. I immersed myself in meditation classes, Reiki, Tarot reading, and all manner of groups and classes designed to get us in touch with who we were and our "purpose". I had a blast learning; experiencing everything. Some of it was deep and profound, others, well, perhaps less so. It's tempting to look back and say, "Geesh, really, how silly?" But, it seemed necessary to do it all, to get in touch with my mystical child - letting her loose in a new way, to explore other ways of being and believing, opening up to the unknown and searching for answers that rang true for me.

Then I heard *The Voice*. In a workshop we were learning to ask questions of our higher-selves and listen for the answers. It wasn't a big voice coming from the heavens, just a small little voice inside that seemed to be speaking profound truth. The answers were simple, but surprising. Things I probably couldn't have made up, if I'd tried. It was during this question and answer session that I discovered/heard/was given my true purpose, "I was to live the love of the universe here on earth".

I don't know about you, but things like that just make me yawn. Seriously, I was here to be *LOVE*? That sounded way out even for me. Love as a purpose had no substance, all airy-fairy, ungrounded and perhaps a bit self-important. Really, who tells themselves they are Love? That seemed arrogant and just plain nonsensical. I mean love? Really?

So what's wrong with being Love, you ask? I thought of love as romance, something made of moonbeams, insipid smiles and, yes I'll admit it, Fake and often manipulative. There were loads of people in the new age world who went around professing, "it's all love, la dee dah". They were *flakes*. It seemed that they had on their rose-colored glasses. They were living in a sing-song fantasy world, ungrounded and insubstantial. I love science fiction and fantasy and spiritual adventures but I don't pretend that most of it is real. This was just too over the top and rather meaningless.

I consulted a psychic, asking her what my purpose was; giving no clue that I might already have received an answer myself. I was dumbfounded when she said almost word for word, "Your purpose is to be the love of the universe here on Earth". I was floored and dismayed. Hey, I wanted a purpose that was meaningful, something like, "Your purpose is to be a Reiki Master, workshop leader, speaker, author, healer...those all seemed to have true meaning and focus. But to just be Love?! Sigh.

Spirituality, for me, is connecting directly with god/goddess/the universe/all-that-is and feeling that energy and love on a very deep and profound level. We can receive/hear messages from the Universe or our higher-selves, and live from a deep place of knowing and connectedness.

Life became simpler in many ways as I allowed spirit to guide me. I "felt" in my heart what was true and right for me. I often experienced the peace that I thought I needed to be a nun to find, a sense of rightness and flow. I felt I was being divinely led from one thing to the next, to the next, even place-to-place to be where I needed to be for the next *whatever*.

I didn't give a lot of thought to my purpose "to be the Love", because, basically I had No idea where to go with that. I just allowed my life to unfold and followed where spirit led. I left a marriage that wasn't bad, but was compressed by his smallness and lack of vision. I'd been keeping part of me small in order to remain. I wanted to expand. I went to the wide-open spaces of Montana. Working with my spiritual teacher who I'll call simply "The Blonde" I went on my own spiritual journey, clearing out old issues, opening to spirit and yes, to love, but not in the sappy romantic way that I'd rejected. Love began to take on a deeper meaning, a depth beyond that which I'd been taught. My heart expanded to take in all of earth and beyond. Yes, I loved individual people, but what I mostly felt was a larger, cosmic type of love that went beyond personality and took in everything as a whole.

In one extremely memorable experience, I was outside meditating in a group with TB (The Blonde), I literally felt my heart expand and take in the whole universe. I felt stretched spiritually and physically. My heart was about to burst out of my chest. TB sat down beside me and asked, "Where is your heart?" In wonder, I answered, "It's everywhere." "Yes it is," she said. My heart became the earth, the universe, and then shattered into millions of pieces that became the stars and became one with all things. I knew what it was to Be Love. I didn't know how to *live* that love on Earth. It was so *far* beyond what I ever imagined. It had nothing to do with "I love you" which often meant things like "you complete me. I need you. I want to own you, be you, control you. I want you to_____fill in your own blanks about what you've demanded love be for you."

I fear a lot of people will misunderstand and take offense at my statement that love is impersonal. I mean that it's not reliant on your actions, your beliefs, your good deeds, and it doesn't go away if you are bad, or sinful. It just IS.

This Love doesn't demand, doesn't request, doesn't give and also doesn't take. It just IS. It is the fabric, the matrix, of the universe. It's what we are, what everything is. It's the energy that we breathe. It's expansive, unconditional and impersonal and it's ours for the…not asking, not taking…it's ours just for opening to it. There is nothing that must be done. Just open to it. Allow it in.

The love we've been taught is far diminished from what I'm talking about. We fear that love can be given and taken away on a whim. We are sure it only comes to us if we are good, perfect, beautiful and amazing. There are many who have lost love, been denied love, or even been wounded or manipulated by trying to be deserving of love. Love has been the cause of much heart-ache and angst. That isn't the love I'm talking about. This is a deeper love and it's not even unconditional; unconditional still implies somehow that you can *have* it or it's given if someone else decides that they'll love you no matter what.

This new type of love is unqualified, unrestricted, unreserved. It has nothing to do with another person. There is nothing you need to do to deserve it – there is nothing you can do that will cause it to be denied or withheld. It just IS and it's yours if you simply open to it.

What I learned for myself is that it's possible to be in that loving energy within seconds. I'd like to say I feel it all the time, and simply move and dance in it knowingly, constantly. But alas, I get caught up in my head, the computer, work, life. I forget to allow myself to simply Be. It's in the moments when I suspend all that I must do and be and allow myself to just relax and breathe that I am once again aware of the depth of love that surrounds me, moving through me, and through all things.

I didn't understand in 2008 when I started making jewelry how significant this choice was going to be for me. My initial desire was to just make "pretty necklaces". That all changed with my first sale.

I'd met a woman at a party who was so excited about what I was doing that she followed me home to look at what else I had made; a total of 4 necklaces. She tried them on, one by one. She picked up one that was nice. I'd worn it and gotten compliments; it was just *nice*. When she put it on, she absolutely transformed. She was glowing and, I swear, so was the necklace. I had tears in my eyes as I felt the power of the energy shift that was occurring. I knew then that somehow this wasn't at all about making something *pretty*, it was about creating powerful jewelry – actually not just jewelry, energy tools. I knew I had to make and share the transformative energy of my creations with others. Bold Bodacious Jewelry was born.

As I worked with the stones and attuned to their vibrations, I was able to see how the energy of the stones helped open the wearer's auric field to allow in those higher frequencies; allowing them to shift into their next level of beingness. These days if someone says "Oh that's so pretty", part of me cringes, because I know they aren't seeing/feeling the energy and power that's present. But, I also know, that they don't have to understand. The magic happens regardless of their awareness.

It wasn't until just now, though, in writing this that I realized that I was being opened up into deeper/higher levels of Love and that is what is "programmed" into each piece that I create. Oh sure, it comes in looking like courage, empowerment, healing, abundance and all those other positive emotions. I honestly believed, until just this minute that's all it was. Not to say that isn't a lot, but this next level is even more exciting.

What is really happening when you put on a Bold Bodacious Creation by me, AnnaMariah, is that your soul, your aura, your body are opening up to Love. It's filling in the places that were closed with the pure energy of Love, the foundation of all-that-is, all that-you-are and will become. In truth, you are becoming more Love, more of who you truly are.

It was a big stretch a couple of years ago when I understood and began to share that when I work with the stones they are returned to the original energy of creation. That seemed like a huge claim to make and took all my courage. Now I'm being asked to take that a step farther and declare my truth on a deeper level than what I'd understood before – the original energy of Creation is Love. Tears run down my face as I feel the power and the truth of my existence.

My purpose to *Live the Love of the Universe on Earth*, has expanded into helping others do the same as I share the jewelry that I make *and* in the sharing of my reality.

Is it possibly *your* purpose to Live the Love of The Universe on Earth as well? Is it the purpose of humanity? Are we all here to experience all that isn't love and finally to come back to a remembering of our true nature – Love? I know that for myself, my writing, my work with gemstones, everything I do and share is, at its foundation is being the energy of this New Love, helping others Re-Member who they are, have been and will be.

No matter what it looks like, what we call it, it's really just Love.

Annamariah Nau is a gemstone intuitive who loves a good story. She's not a picky reader, but she's always looking for stories that offer hope and truth and maybe just a touch of magic. She says "sometimes all it takes to believe in yourself is to see that you aren't the only one". When she isn't writing in the middle of the night or in off the wall locations, Annamariah designs one of a kind gemstone jewelry for her company Bold Bodacious Jewelry. She has a wandering nature and has lived all over the US. She and her husband, David, a designer and watercolor artist, are currently based in Virginia and waiting to see where their next adventure will take them.

Live outside the box, sing, dance, love, laugh, be fully you with the power of Bold Bodacious gemstone jewelry.
AnnaMariahNau@gmail.com
www.boldbodaciousjewelry.com

Heal My Voice Projects

www.healmyvoice.org

Join us in our mission to help each woman discover her voice:

Heal My Voice empowers and supports women and girls globally to heal, reclaim their voice and step into greater leadership in their lives and in the world.

Your Voice Matters!

TO ORDER additional copies of this book and to discover additional Heal My Voice books in this series and current programs, go to the Heal My Voice website:

www.HealMyVoice.org

Healing Circle: Meditation and Energy Clearing-Tele-seminar Style:

Energy tools shared during a 30 minute meditation.

Sign up for newsletter on the website: www.healmyvoice.org

Go to **www.healmyvoice.org** for the latest up to date news and projects.

Heal My Voice Book Series

Fearless Voices:
True Stories by Courageous Women

Empowered Voices:
True Stories by Awakened Women

Inspired Voices:
True Stories by Visionary Women

Harmonic Voices:
True Stories by Women on the Path to Peace

Words from Alan Peterson

First Heal My Voice Fundraiser

May 11, 2011

Healing the Voice

Since the beginning of time we have added our voice to the celestial chorus that fills the heavens and earth. Upon the agreement with our birth mother we transformed from the spiritual to the human. Our voices changed and our needs changed, but our spirit did not. Over "time" we have had different platforms on which to stand and speak our truth and express our voice.

At first it was the baby's coo and cry. And as we grew, parents and society tried to curb and shape our voice to fit someone elses beliefs. Through it all we have continued to grow, expand and develop our own voice in the world. Sometimes, we have been hurt deeply by ourselves and others. So much so that our voices are stilled and shut down.

In each of us there is that spirit, that knowledge of the choir we all sang with, that reminds us of who we are and where we come from. It is the antidote for silence, the elixir for songlessness. It is the same energy that inspires great works of art and musical masterpieces, great inventions and expanded philosophies. It is the calling of the soul, the song of the spirit, the great healing of the heart and voice.

Like the newborn babe learning to speak we awaken from our slumber to a new day and we create the light of that day by shining our spirit on ourselves and others. It is the light of the Divine Feminine, the mother of us all calling, soothing, loving, nurturing, teaching, encouraging us to sing, and healing us with love, the love that is the center of all life. To know that we are not alone, that we are worthy of love, that with love, in love and through love we can raise our voices to the sky, sing, shout, and feel free to let it all come out! We are free, we are magnificent we are beautiful. Like the phoenix we rise and soar in the heavens beyond the stars. Like the newborn we giggle and cry then grow up to speak our truth for all to hear. Like the new disciple who has discovered her faith, we shout it from the mountain top, born again - remembering of who we are.

Love.

Alan Peterson Musician and songwriter Alan Peterson uses the transformative power of music and lyrics, to uncover the truths that lay deep within the heart. Alan's playful, positive and sometimes rebellious approach provides a soundtrack to the soul, facilitating an experience that empowers audiences to create deeper, more meaningful and joyous lives. In Alan's words:

"My desire is to share music that creates a bridge to a deeper experience of One love. I believe that love IS the answer, and I want people to feel that, know it, take it. And, then, to go out and play."

Love Resources

Love in Action

Books
Songs
Blogtalk Radio Shows

We encourage you to use the blank pages throughout this book to write your stories, reflections and Love in Action Inspirations.

Books

- Madly in Love with ME, the Daring Adventure to Becoming Your Own Best Friend by Christine Arylo

- Living From the Heart: Heart Rhythm Meditation for Energy, Clarity, Peace, Joy and Inner Power by Puran Bair

- Living, Loving and Learning by Leo Buscaglia

- The Artist's Way by Julia Cameron

- The Alchemist Paolo Coelho

- You Can Heal Your Life by Louise Hay

- Getting the Love You Want by Harville Hendrix

- Loving What Is: Four Questions That Can Change Your Life by Byron Katie

- The Art of Forgiveness, Loving-kindness and Peace by Jack Kornfield

- Broken Open~How Difficult Times Can Help Us Grow by Elizabeth Lesser

- The Intention Experiment by Lynne McTaggart

- Compassion: The Ultimate Flowering of Love by Osho

- First Invite Love In: 40 Time-Tested Tools For Creating A More Compassionate Life by Tana Pesso with Penor Rinpoche

- The Heart's Unraveling Chamber One: The Birth of a New Evolutionary Directive by Maria Lucia Picaza

- The Celestine Prophecy by James Redfield

- Women, Food and God by Geneen Roth

- The Four Agreements by Don Miguel Ruiz

- Course in Miracles by Helen Schucman and William Thetford

- I Dare to Heal With Compassionate Love by Joel Vorensky

- A Return to Love by Marianne Williamson

Love Songs

- All You Need is Love The Beatles

- Trust Love Rickie Byars Beckwith

- Light My Fire – The Doors

- Love is an Open Door: Frozen Soundtrack

- Ain't No Mountain High Enough- Marvin Gaye and Tammi Terrell

- When Love Takes Over - David Guetta (feat. Kelly Rowland)

- Good Night My Love Honor Society

- Man in the Mirror Michael Jackson

- Can You Feel the Love Tonight Elton John

- LoveBug The Jonas Brothers

- Silly Love Songs- Paul McCartney

- I Like It, I Love It Tim McGraw
- Love Someone: Jason Mraz

- Circle of Love Alan Peterson

- You're the Top Cole Porter

- Lovin' You: Minnie Riperton

- How Could Anyone – Libby Roderick

- Let My Love Open the Door: Pete Townshend

- Give Love MC Yogi

Love Inspired:
Heal My Voice Blogtalk Radio Shows

Voices of Love: Lessons from an Earth Angel
Jannirose JOY, guest
March 19, 2013

Liz & Andrea talk with **Jannirose JOY** about the lessons she learns about love from her son Charlie who was born with Down syndrome. March 21st is World Down Syndrome Day - Tri-somy 21 means 3 copies of the 21st chromosome in every cell)

http://www.blogtalkradio.com/healmyvoice/2013/03/19/voices-of-love--lessons-from-an-earth-angel-1

♫♪♫♪•*¨`*•.,.,♫♪,.,.•*¨`*•♫♪

Voices of Love: The Inspiration of Your Brilliant Voice
Liz Draman and Andrea Hylen Conversation
March 26, 2013

What inspiration is your brilliant voice bringing to you? Do you hear the inspiration? How we listen, receive and take action from Inspiration! Call in for light-speed coaching and Awaken Your Brilliant Voice!

http://www.blogtalkradio.com/healmyvoice/2013/03/26/voices-of-love-the-inspiration-of-your-brilliant-voice-1

♫♪♪♫•*¨¨*•.‚ ‚♫♪‚ ‚.•*¨¨*•♫♪

Voices of Love: On Purpose Woman
Ginny Robertson, guest
April 2, 2013

Ginny Robertson is the Founder of On Purpose Woman and Editor/Publisher of the FREE Publication On Purpose Woman Magazine. This was an inspirational conversation about Ginny's inspiration to gather women together in a supportive community and network with a feminine style and the inspiration to honor a woman each year as a Woman of Purpose. (Andrea is the 2013 Woman of Purpose.)

http://www.blogtalkradio.com/healmyvoice/2013/04/02/voices-of-love-on-purpose-woman-ginny-robertson

♫♪♪♫•*¨¨*•.‚ ‚♫♪‚ ‚.•*¨¨*•♫♪

Voices of Love: A Conversation with Liz and Andrea
Occupy Love film, Astrology, Life
April 23, 2013

Love, Astrology, some of the ways we support ourselves and others in this time of constant flux and stay connected to Love. And a shout out to the Film Occupy LOVE.

http://www.blogtalkradio.com/healmyvoice/2013/04/23/voices-of-love-a-conversation-with-liz-and-andrea

♫♪♫•*¨*•.¸¸♫♪¸¸.•*¨*•♫♪

Voices of Love; Dare to Fall in Love With Yourself
Christine Arylo, guest
June 25, 2013

Dare to Fall in Love... with yourself. Make your relationship with yourself the best relationship of your life. Join best-selling author of the book Madly in Love with ME, the Daring Adventure to Becoming Your Own Best Friend, Christine Arylo, and go beyond the idea of loving yourself, into the real how-to love yourself in all ways, every day. Using her breakthrough love-ology "The 10 Branches of Self Love" you'll learn the difference between self-compassion, self-esteem, self-worth, self-care and more, and take a "Self-Love Pulse Check" to see what kind of love you need most this year. Christine Arylo, m.b.a, is an inspirational catalyst and internationally recognized speaker and best-selling author who teaches people how to put their most important partnership first, the one with themselves, so that they can create the life their hearts and souls crave.

http://www.blogtalkradio.com/healmyvoice/2013/06/25/voices-of-love--dare-to-fall-in-love-with-yourself

♫♪♪♫•*¨¨*•., ,♫♪, ,.•*¨¨*•♫♪

Voices of Love: Write Your Juice. Live Your Joy
Lisa McCourt, guest
July 2, 2013

Talking about joy . . . the kind of day-to-day, consistent joy that depends upon radical authenticity and outrageous self-love. Only through those two critical pathways can Juicy Joy be reached and maintained. Lisa will show us how to access the Juicy Joyful state through writing and creative expression. Lisa is both a writing coach and a joy-trainer, and she will demonstrate how those two seemingly-different occupations are closely intertwined.

http://www.blogtalkradio.com/healmyvoice/2013/07/02/voices-of-love-write-your-juice--live-your-joy

♫♪♪♫•*¨¨*•., ,♫♪, ,.•*¨¨*•♫♪

Voices of Love from Mother Earth
Mare Cromwell Guest
July 9, 2013

Mare Cromwell is the author of Messages from Mother...Earth Mother. Powerful, sacred conversation of Love. She is Mother. Earth Mother. She is the ground we stand on. She is the powerful Planetary Caretaker who birthed evolution into existence on this planet. She is the one who dreamed all the fishes in the ocean, the trees, the plants, the four-leggeds, even us two-leggeds into existence. Along with the Great Mystery/God/Allah/Creator. (Choose your term.) All planets have Planetary Caretakers. This one, Earth, happens to be female. Some Planetary Caretakers are male, such as Mars. There is more to her than words can describe. Especially English words since our language is missing terms that can truly go into detail about her and what she is about. Most native tongues have words in their languages that can better describe her. And she's been forgotten, for the most part. Sigh...

http://www.blogtalkradio.com/healmyvoice/2013/07/09/voices-of-love-messages-from-motherearth-mother

♫♪♪♫•*¨*•.₎ ₎♫♪₎ ₎.•*¨*•♫♪

Bringing Your Gifts to the World
Marie ek Lipanovska, guest
July 16, 2014

A conversation with Marie ek Lipanovska, the founder of Heal My Voice Sweden and Liz Draman, Awaken to Love

http://www.blogtalkradio.com/healmyvoice/2013/07/16/bring

ing-your-gifts-to-the-world

♫♪♪♫•*¨¨*•.₎ ₎♫♪₎ ₎.•*¨¨*•♫♪

Freedom From Abuse: Choosing to Receive Love
Jacke Schroeder, guest
April 28, 2014

Jacke Schroeder is an author, speaker and spiritual business consultant. She joins Andrea Hylen for a conversation about Freedom from Abuse and choosing to receive love. When people have been abused it takes a devastating toll on their ability to share in intimate relationships. Facing the truth releases the shame and opens the way to receive love.

http://www.blogtalkradio.com/healmyvoice/2014/04/28/freed
om-from-abuse-choosing-to-receive-love

♫♪♪♫•*¨¨*•.₎ ₎♫♪₎ ₎.•*¨¨*•♫♪

May is for Metta: A Journey in Loving Kindness
Beth Terrence, guest
April 26, 2014

Beth Terrence joins Andrea Hylen for a conversation about the 4th annual May Is For Metta: 31 Days Of Loving-kindness Exploration **May Is For Metta is a gathering of a virtual**

sangha (community) with participants from all over the world energetically coming together for daily guided meditation practice and exploration during the month of May. The intention is to cultivate greater loving-kindness and compassion for ourselves, others and the world.

http://www.blogtalkradio.com/healmyvoice/2014/04/26/may-is-for-metta-a-journey-in-loving-kindness